Emerging Son

Emerging Son

A memoir
By Tom Bengtson

Emerging Son

First edition
First printing
September 2004

Published by:
NFR Communications, Inc.
7614 York Avenue South, No. 3314
Minneapolis, Minnesota 55435

Library of Congress Control Number:
2004094378

Cover art by Margaret Schmit

ISBN: 0-9754134-0-6

Printed in Rochester, Minnesota
United States of America

Susan:

Emerging Son is dedicated to you.

Tom

Acknowledgements

Emerging Son grew out of the inspiration of several people; five merit particular acknowledgement.

First is Jackie Hilgert, my dear friend who encouraged me in June of 1999 to take on this project. Her suggestions and support were invaluable.

Second is Marc Nieson, who explained memoir to me and coached me through draft after draft. He helped me to appreciate the craft of storytelling and taught me a lot about how to tell my own story.

Third is my wife, Susan. Ever since I have known her, she has nurtured my aspirations to write. I could not have written *Emerging Son* without her love.

Finally, I have to acknowledge my father and mother, Frank and Rose Anne Bengtson, who gave me a wonderful childhood. I would have no story to tell at all if it were not for these magnificent parents.

Emerging Son

Introduction

My father always seemed happy at home and I thought I wanted to be the same way. Independent and certain, Dad did things his way while I wondered if I'd ever find my way. They call imitation the greatest form of flattery and I wonder if that's because it's so difficult. Can a man who grew up in the 1960s and 1970s reflect the life of a man who grew up in the 1930s and 1940s? Times change so much. Dad was clearly at home in his era. I wasn't so sure about me in mine.

In the early 1980s, when I was still in college, Dad invited me to the Boat Show in downtown Minneapolis as he had so many times when I was a kid. This time we went to see Gerry Spiess, the adventurous Minnesotan who had won fame by sailing solo across the ocean in a 10-foot boat called the *Yankee Girl*. Now he was on the show circuit, meeting fans like my Dad and me, explaining how he did it.

"The *Yankee Girl* wasn't too small," Spiess responded to a question. "I knew I could handle everything on that boat by myself. Once, the mast came down. I was able to re-step it by myself. If I had been on a bigger boat, my voyage would have been over."

The message resonated with Dad, who also liked to handle things by himself. He always solved his own problems. And, like Spiess, he wasn't concerned about size nor about impressing others. He simply knew what worked for him and took pride in not having to ask anyone for help.

Frank Alexander Bengtson was born in Minneapolis a month before the stock market crashed in 1929. His father, my grandfather, sold insurance and died when Frank was 12. Dad says he doesn't remember much about his father, except that he taught him to play golf. Dad was left-handed but he learned to play right-handed because his father's clubs were the only ones available. In a subtler lesson, Dad may have taken note of his father's schedule, which must have offered flexibility unknown to people who punch a clock five days a week.

Fate unfolded along my Dad's interests. He studied to become a schoolteacher, yet while attending the University of Minnesota, he helped his mother with the tax issues she inherited along with some property in Wisconsin. Later, she turned the whole thing – building and tax bills – over to him and he quickly saw the benefits of property management. Over the next three decades, he bought and sold apartment buildings, initially during the summers he had off from teaching. By the time he was approaching 40, he left teaching to devote himself full-time to housing.

Drawing on his experience as an industrial arts teacher and property manager, Dad made our south Minneapolis house a home and I thought it was paradise. Located a few miles from where Dad grew up, the house was filled with furniture Dad made — a coffee table, two end tables, a TV stand, and lots of shelves for books and toys. Using his own drawings and a lot of elbow grease, Dad converted the upstairs of the house from a marginally useful storage space to a full floor with two bedrooms that housed my three sisters, my brother, and me.

We had a yard and an alley to play in. Dad taught all of us how to throw and hit a baseball; he put up a basketball hoop in the driveway and he took us camping. Dad showed us how to work a compass and how to fish. He took us to state parks and to the North Shore but we could have camped anywhere as we towed behind us a little trailer that featured a stove and two beds.

Imitating Dad, I gravitated toward individual pursuits. I played tennis and chess, and I started my own newspaper in high school. Dad encouraged me to make my own employment and I got started early, seeking household painting work in the neighborhood when I was a teen. I really liked the work and I made pretty good money at it, much of it coming from Dad who paid me to paint the window trim on his apartment buildings.

Dad was proud of the buildings he managed and I was proud to have a maintenance role in the family business. Once, Dad took me on a drive and pointed out the first fourplex he ever owned. It was a dumpy looking building but Dad saw opportunity in it, despite the rather bleak neighborhood. "The building looked the same way when I bought it years ago," Dad told me. "I looked at that building back then and said, 'that fourplex was there long before I came along and it will probably be there long after I'm gone. Someone is going to be collecting rent on that property and it may as well be me.'"

Dad built a business on that philosophy, a business that gave him the freedom he wanted and the income to give a wife and five kids a pretty good life. His do-it-yourself approach worked because Dad was willing to put in a lot of his own sweat equity. He fixed things on his own, painted and replaced carpeting without much help, even plowed the parking lots of snow. But this business style had its limitations. By his middle 40s, Dad reached the capacity of his management load and the business remained a steady size until he began selling a decade later in preparation for retirement.

Looking at my Gerry Spiess autograph, I asked Dad a question on the way home from the Boat Show. "Why don't you expand your business … get more property? Don't you want more?"

"I know my limits," Dad said. "I could take on a partner and expand, but I decided a long time ago that I wanted a business where I could handle everything on my own."

I nodded, thinking Dad was the smartest man in the world. I wondered if I'd ever be that smart.

1

Sailing Lessons

The Boat Show was like a warm sunny day at the lake in the middle of winter. That's the conclusion I drew when Dad took me to the Minneapolis Auditorium that January when I was barely a teenager, beginning an annual ritual. Dad always ignored the yachts and runabouts, and headed straight for the sailboats. He spent a lot of time examining the masts and sails, and climbing in and out of each cockpit. He would run his hand along the deck on boats with wood finishes. He worked the tiller on a big Catalina and compared it to the wheel on an Islander. He asked a salesman about the ballast in the keel, the composition of the hull, and the square footage of the mainsail. I tagged along, like an eager student might follow an esteemed professor in a museum. To me, all the sailboats looked the same; Dad taught me otherwise.

"Look at the shape of the hull," he told me.

Differences began to emerge. Some of the sailboats

had bottoms shaped like teardrops, coming to a point in the center. Others had flat bottoms; those were called scows. And still others – catamarans – had two hulls that looked like a pair of bananas. The tops of the hulls were equally varied. Some had little cabins that accommodated a bed and lunch table. Others barely had room for two people to put their feet. Some had splash breaks and railings, or compartments for storage, or hatch covers, or a place for sunbathing. Still others were no more complex than a rowboat.

"Look at the sails," Dad said.

All the sailboats had big sails with a mast and boom but that's where the similarity stopped. Some of the mainsails had a pronounced outward curve that required the use of sticks or "batons" to hold their shape. Other mainsails were more triangular with sharp, straight edges. Some of the boats had a sail in front of the mast, called a jib. And still others had a third sail called a spinnaker. There were even some boats with two masts.

"Notice the different sizes," Dad said.

Sure enough, sailboats came in all sizes – small ones that couldn't be sailed without getting wet. Big ones that looked spacious enough to live on. Thin ones that looked as though they could race through the water like a dolphin. And there were fat boats that looked like they were made for family barbecues on the water. Some of the boats were so cumbersome they could only be hoisted into the water with a crane. Others were light enough to strap to the top of a station wagon.

Once Dad taught me how to look at sailboats, I began to see a lot of things I hadn't noticed before.

* * *

Growing up, we lived just a few blocks from Lake Nokomis, a long body of water sliced on one end by the Cedar Avenue Bridge. Parkland surrounds the lake and, as kids, this was where we skated, rode our bicycles, played softball, and learned to swim.

Lake Nokomis had about 100 buoys for sailboats near its west shore. Boat owners rented the buoys for the summer, beginning about May. Dad spent a lot of time looking at the boats and so did I. The halyards, clanging against the masts of the boats, called like free samples at the candy store. I watched the sailors rig their boats at the dock, taking note of the ropes and pulleys and mooring chains and cranks and hooks and stopwatches.

When we would go to Nokomis to play ball, I would always take a few extra minutes to check out the sailing area. During the week it was quiet, the majestic scows floating on the mirrorlike lake as if they were swans in a deep sleep. Most of the boats were protected by a canvas tarp, which prevented me from seeing inside the cockpit. Some were splattered with bird droppings but the ones that protected against this hazard with a plastic owl perched near the top of the mast looked clean. I'd read the names across the transom: *Sunshine*, *Getaway*, *Lady Luck*, *Son of the Beach* and *Wet Dreams*.

Calypso was the name of a boat my friend sailed. Myron Orfield, the youngest of six children, lived across the street from Lake Nokomis and his family owned a Johnson M scow, a beautiful 16-foot boat with a jib and twin, inboard rudders. Myron was one of my best friends from Resurrection Grade School and during the summer between sixth and seventh grades, he took me sailing on the *Calypso*. Having sailed from infancy, Myron was a good sailor by the time he gave me my first ride on a sailboat. We rowed the tender to his boat where I dropped him off and returned the rowboat to shore. In the meantime, he rigged the *Calypso* at its mooring and sailed it to the dock where he picked me up. I sat near the front of the cockpit while Myron stepped off the dock and into the boat, giving us a little momentum to begin our reach across the lake.

Myron told me to watch out for the boom, the heavy beam that secured the bottom of the mainsail. On the *Calypso*, the boom was made of wood and could easily have knocked an unsuspecting person unconscious. Myron let me control the jib, pulling and securing the appropriate lines on his command. He showed me how the boat responded to even slight movements of the tiller and mainsheet. I watched the painter off the bow flop in the water as we sailed and came about.

Most impressive to me was the way Myron could make the boat heel. With a certain wind, Myron could trim the mainsheet in such a way that the hull underneath us would rise out of the water. The boat was leaning over and I thought we were going to capsize. As the hull under our seats rose, we arched back, locking our feet under the lip of the cockpit. We used our weight to counterbalance the boat, which seemed to be tipping into the water below us. The mast followed, reaching almost parallel to the surface of the water. Sometimes Myron would let the mainsheet out a little and the end of the boom would dip into the lake. I looked behind me and saw the bottom of the *Calypso*, the high-side sideboard protruding three feet into the air. To the uninitiated, it seemed nuts but Myron knew what he was doing. We didn't capsize. We didn't even get wet. This was the thrill of sailing, pushing the limits of the boat and your skills. I thought it was fantastic and I accepted every sailing invitation Myron ever extended.

✳ ✳ ✳

One winter in the mid-1970s – I must have been about 14 — Dad returned from the Boat Show with an announcement.

"I've bought a sailboat."

Wow! I thought. Our very own sailboat!

Dad showed us a picture of the boat, which was

called the *Wildflower*. It was black with a white deck and a big orange W on the mainsail. I had never seen a sailboat with a black hull before but it looked sporty in the picture. The *Wildflower* was 12 feet long and shaped like a rowboat with a square bow. It was made of a kind of heavy-duty Styrofoam and it had a teak bench with a centerboard through the middle. The aluminum mast reached probably 16 feet in the air and there was a small jib. The picture showed the boat with a colorful spinnaker but our boat didn't come with one.

Dad arranged to lease one of those buoys on Lake Nokomis and when spring came we prepared to launch the boat. We took about an hour to step the mast according to the instructions that came with the boat; then we had to learn about the rigging. It took us probably another hour to figure out how to attach each of the sails and how to thread the ropes through the various pulleys. We were surprised by the buoyancy of the *Wildflower*, which sat remarkably high in the water, even with people in it. No more than a few inches of the hull disappeared below the waterline. It was a relatively flat, wide boat, a design that seemed to accentuate the impact of Lake Nokomis' small waves.

Dad agreed to let me invite Myron on our maiden outing. None of us really knew how to sail, so I figured it would make sense to have Myron take us out. Myron readily agreed. With the *Wildflower* rigged for action and tethered to the sailing dock, the Bengtson family of seven and Myron gathered for the inaugural voyage. Dad brought life preservers, the bright orange kind that wrap around your neck, significantly limiting the mobility of your head. Mom refused to get in the boat. Unable to swim, Mom had never liked boats much anyway, and the *Wildflower* appeared too unstable to fit within the limits of her comfort zone.

Dad loaded the five of us kids in the boat. Three sat on the center bench and two sat near the mast, trying to stay out of the jib's way. Myron and Dad sat at the stern where they had the best access to the tiller and mainsheet. After two hours of build-up, we had attracted a small crowd of strangers on shore for our launch. Mom stood in the center of the group, arms folded as she watched us take off. One of us in the boat lifted the painter over the dock post and pushed the bow of the boat toward the center of the lake. In an instant, wind filled our mainsail and we were moving. Even with seven people in the boat, the *Wildflower* moved at a pretty good clip.

Myron tugged on the mainsheet and said he was going to "see what she could do." Dad urged caution. Myron reassured Dad and got the *Wildflower* to heel. Water started to flow into the cockpit over a wide spot on the low side of the hull. Myron ignored it and kept pulling, trying to get the boat to heel even farther. But the *Wildflower* was not built like the *Calypso*. It was designed to sail on its belly, not on its side. We had been sailing only a few minutes when Myron passed the point of no return and we began to tip. When Myron realized what was happening, he let go of the mainsheet but it was too late. Once the *Wildflower* started to tip, there was no stopping her. The boat went over onto its side, the mainsail floating along the top of the water. Everyone fell into the cold water, although our life vests kept us floating. I caught a glimpse of my horrified mother on shore, her worst fears about sailing realized before her eyes.

The *Wildflower* wasn't done yet. As the hull continued to take on water, the boat began to turtle. The mast disappeared into the lake and the whalelike bottom of the boat rose up out of the water. The mast was pointing straight down to the bottom of the lake as our gloves, caps and coins sank out of reach. Dad frantically counted heads. He readily noted five bobbing figures, which was one less than he needed. "Where was Tom?" he thought. I had emerged in a cavity under the hull. No one could see me but I had a unique view of the inside of the Wildflower with its rigging upset, its dagger-board falling in and its tiller popping out of its mount.

A man on shore quickly rowed one of the tender boats to us and plucked all of us out of the water, including me after I swam out to where everyone could see me. Our rescuer returned the soaking wet kids to Mom, who took us to our car where the heater prevented us from catching cold. Dad stayed to right the boat, a task that ultimately required the use of two tender boats. Although we were only about 25 feet from the sailing dock, Dad said we were fortunate to be out far enough from shore that the mast did not lodge in the lake's muddy bottom.

* * *

Despite the rocky start, sailing proved to be a wonderful father-and-son hobby. The others sailed but over the next two summers, it was Dad and me who spent the most time on the *Wildflower*. Eventually, we figured out how to sail on our own. We learned how to reach and run and come about and jibe and cast off and land. By summer's end, I was slaloming around the buoys and the boats moored to them.

Sailing taught me to pay attention to details. Sailing is about harnessing the wind, and to make the most of it a sailor has to know what the wind is doing. I learned to watch the surface of the lake, which offers many clues. Waves can indicate the direction and intensity of the wind, and most important, warn you about dead spots where there is no wind. I had seen my dad wet the end of his finger and hold it in the air to determine the wind's direction, but I wanted something more telling so we tied pieces of yarn on two of the halyards about six feet up from the deck. I glanced at these telltales every few seconds as I captained the *Wildflower*, constantly reassessing the wind. I was surprised to learn how often the wind changes direction. If I failed to watch closely, sometimes the wind would shift so violently that the boom would jump from one side of the cockpit to the other, almost knocking me over. Small indicators can foretell big changes.

As a new sailor, I was intrigued by the way a sailboat gets from one spot to another. I learned that if you want to go from point A to point B, sometimes you have to sail toward point C for a little while. If my destination was directly upwind, I had to do something called "tacking," which is the process of sailing in a zigzag pattern to get from a downwind spot to an upwind spot. The captain needs to figure out how many tacks to make and how steep to make each tack. Sailing races are won and lost on these decisions. In sailing, you have to work with nature; an experienced sailor knows that the path that seems obvious to the novice isn't always the best way to go.

I grew in confidence that first summer with the *Wildflower* and by August felt proficient enough to invite Myron for a ride — only this time with me at the helm. We sailed around the lake and Myron may have grown a little bored as the *Wildflower* clearly was not as fast as the *Calypso*. But the boredom ended in an instant when the *Wildflower's* mast keeled over without warning. "What the …?!" I thought, examining the rigging that was supposed to hold the mast in place. It didn't take long before we figured out a cotter pin had slipped free, releasing one of the halyards.

Fortunately, we weren't too far from shore, so we paddled to land and pulled the *Wildflower* up onto a beach. We were on the opposite side of the lake from our launch point however, and we didn't have another cotter pin. I suggested one of us wait with the boat while the other jog back to the sailing area to get a tender boat. One of us could row across the lake and then tow the *Wildflower* back to the sailing dock where we could get another cotter pin and re-step the mast. Myron said he had a better idea: we should flag down the lake ranger and get him to tow us back to the sailing dock. The lake ranger was a college-age boy in a fishing boat with a 10-horse motor and a whistle around his neck. He spent most of the summer hollering at kids who attempted to swim across the lake or dive off of one of the lake's fishing docks. I followed Myron's advice but I felt guilty relying on someone else to solve my problem.

Early October brought the end of the sailing season and the close of the best summer I had ever had. That funny little black boat was my ticket to the good life. I thought sailing was better than anything at school or my bike or Little League or even television. After helping Dad pack the boat away in our backyard for the winter, I asked him how many days until spring.

"Too many," Dad said. "Too many."

* * *

Two Boat Shows later, Dad came home with another announcement:

"I have traded the *Wildflower* in for a new boat."

We rushed outside to behold a beautiful boat with a white hull and red deck. It was a 16-foot scow with an aluminum mast and boom that were painted black. A teak splash-break popped out of the deck just before the mast; bailers on the floor of the cockpit promised to keep our feet dry, and the outboard tiller, with its aluminum extender, screamed for someone to take hold of her. The boat had just one sail, but what a sail! The mast was 24 feet high and the sail curved outward to catch as much wind as possible. The flat-bottom hull with its two metal sideboards was designed for speed. This was a first-class boat that would roar through the water as fast as anything on Lake Nokomis.

As spring approached, I couldn't wait to put the new boat in the water. Dad named her *Rose Anne* over the objections of my Mom, who said she was unlikely to ever take a ride in the boat. Nonetheless, Dad tenderly painted the name in black lettering across the transom.

❋ ❋ ❋

We opened the sailing season that year like we had before – in the community room at one of the city parks. Early each spring, the Minneapolis Park Board conducted a lottery for the buoys on the lakes. During the winter, sailboat owners registered with the Park Board to get in on the drawing. As the names were pulled from a hat, boat owners got to choose the buoy they wanted for the summer. If you didn't show up for the drawing, the Park Board gave you whatever buoy was left over at the end of the lottery. These were the worst buoys on the lake, the ones farthest from the sailing dock requiring the longest tender boat ride. Dad and I considered the acquisition of a well-placed buoy to be absolutely essential to having a good summer. Attendance at the lottery was very important and we prayed for weeks leading up to the event that our names would be drawn early. On our way to the lottery that evening, neither of us said a word. Our fate lay before us and there was nothing we could do about it.

We arrived to a crowded room and the drawing soon began. The first name was announced and it was not ours. The winner leapt out of his chair and raced up to the map displayed at the front of the room. The lucky sailor drove a pin through the best buoy on the lake – No. 1, located only a few feet from the sailing dock. His summer in paradise was set; he'd get all the benefits of a city lake mooring without much of the work. More names were drawn and happy boat owners eagerly claimed their prize positions on the lake. Sometimes the moderator drew the name of a no-show. "He'll be sorry," my dad muttered just loud enough for me to hear.

Finally the man drawing the names called "Frank Bengtson." Dad and I rushed to the front of the room and selected a buoy in the middle of the pack. The one we got was far enough from shore that we wouldn't have to worry about fishermen casting into our boat, yet close enough to the dock that we wouldn't wear ourselves out rowing to and from our boat. With a decent buoy placement, I figured we could have a pretty good summer.

The *Rose Anne* proved easy to sail and like Myron's boat, it was designed to heel. On a good run, the high side of the hull would rise out of the water and the boat would pick up speed. I learned just how far I could push the *Rose Anne* before she would begin to lose speed and even tip over. In fact, I eventually learned to  tip the boat on purpose and right it by myself without getting wet. As the boat was going over, I'd climb over the high side of the hull and stand on the sideboard. My weight would reverse the momentum of the boat and she would begin to right. As the mast came up out of the water, I'd climb back into the cockpit, my foot leaving the sideboard just as the hull would come crashing back on top of the water. Dad was so impressed by this little maneuver that he asked me to do it in front of the sailing dock where he captured it on film with his Super-8 movie camera.

Sailing brought me life. The sound and smell of the lake water mixed with the warmth of the sun on my lean teenage body and made me high. A city lake is a wonderful place for a teen to be in the summer. How many people were watching the *Rose Anne* from shore, perhaps a little jealous? How many were looking at me, this kid who happened to be lucky enough to have a dad bit by the sailing bug? Maybe no one, in fact, but in my mind it was everyone and I liked the celebrity status. I liked that I could sail the boat by myself. I wasn't dependent upon someone else.

Melanie, my high school sweetheart, came from a sailing family, her father keeping a boat on a large lake west of the cities. The first time I took her sailing on Lake Nokomis she wore a yellow, two-piece bathing suit. She knew how to sail, moving from one side of the boat to the other, depending on the wind. Another time, Melanie and her parents took me sailing on their lake. I would hate to have to choose between a girlfriend and a sailboat but that summer I had both and it seemed like heaven.

Myron and I would sometimes race, as the *Calypso* and the *Rose Anne* were evenly matched. The *Calypso* had a jib but the *Rose Anne* had a slightly bigger mainsail. Myron and I would sail along, our boats only a foot or two apart. The upwind boat had a slight advantage if it was positioned directly in the path of the wind for the other boat. If you could steal the wind from the downwind boat, it would lose speed and the upwind boat could race ahead. Sometimes we devised a racecourse made up of several legs. The trick was to figure out how to complete the course with as few tacks as possible. While Myron and I might start out with our boats a few feet apart, we often ended up on opposite sides of the lake by the middle of the race depending on where each of us decided to turn for a new tack.

Although a sailor is completely dependent upon the wind, I found that a good afternoon of sailing actually has very little to do with the wind. I had fun regardless of whether the wind was whistling at 15 miles an hour or barely stirring. Apparently, it's not so much the power of the wind that matters but what you do with it.

I don't know if Dad ever realized how much his investment in a sailboat paid off for me. Sailing taught me lessons at a young age that I have carried with me all my life. You can't control the wind, and the best sailors don't complain about it. They focus on the things they can control, making adjustments that help make the most of their situation. Sometimes, a sailor encounters an unexpected shift in the wind that other sailors avoid. Yet, if you react to the shift correctly, it doesn't always slow you down. It may, in fact, prove to be just what you need.

2

Apprenticeship

Upon graduation from college in 1983, this lifelong Minnesotan thought home might be somewhere else. Although I loved my parents, I didn't want to live with them as I had while attending the University of Minnesota studying journalism. In fact, I thought I needed to get far away. None of us kids had done that. Terri and Peggy, my two older sisters, stayed in the Twin Cities after their post-high school education; my younger brother, Bob, was still at the U of M. And, although my youngest sister Jeanne was away for college, she was barely across the border in Wisconsin. I was eager to be the first to *really* leave the nest. A classified advertisement in a media trade magazine said there was an opening at a small newspaper in upstate New York. I applied, and after one telephone interview, got the job.

I arrived on a mid-July afternoon at the Tri-Lakes regional airport in the heart of the Adirondack Mountains where the sports editor's job awaited me at the

Apprenticeship

Adirondack Daily Enterprise. Charlie Decker, a lumber-jack of a man who worked his way to the No. 2 position at the *Enterprise*, picked me up and welcomed me to Saranac Lake. I soaked in the airport's surroundings, fixating initially on a dispensing box that displayed that day's edition of the newspaper. Decker pulled out a quarter and bought me a copy, the first I'd ever seen. I immediately turned to the back of the newspaper where I found a three-page sports section. Those three broad sheets looked like an awful lot of space to fill every day.

The drive from the airport took us through dense forest and by glistening lakes, like something you'd see in a vacation brochure. Lakes sparkled everywhere – lakes that Decker told me were devoid of fish due to acidity from air pollution that blew down from Montreal. But the acidity of the region evaded me. These mountains looked tremendous to a guy who grew up in the plains. The scent of pine hung in the air; with so little traffic and even less noise it was easy to forget that people actually lived here.

The trees and lakes reminded me of my youth when Dad would take us camping. The Adirondacks were a little like the Black Hills, I thought. The view from the forested elevations brought a certain peacefulness, the same feeling I remember having as a kid when our family vacationed in South Dakota. Dad made us feel at home in nature, telling us stories around the campfire, showing us the differences between one tree and another, and demonstrating the fine art of filleting fish we caught out of the lake. Maybe my time in the Adirondacks would be like back then. I'd listen to the locals for stories, which I'd retell in the newspaper. And I'd try to pay attention to the little things in my surroundings.

One of the first things to notice was the geography of the region, some 50 miles west of the state's border with Vermont. The local map showed three towns: Tupper Lake, Saranac Lake, and Lake Placid, the town that brought fame to the area by hosting the Winter Olympic Games in 1932 and 1980. I would be living in Saranac Lake where the *Enterprise* had its office, a one-story building with a large satellite dish affixed to the roof. Entering the building through a back door, Decker showed me the office and introduced me to the publisher, who'd hired me sight unseen. Wearing skintight biking shorts, Mr. William Doolittle was munching vigorously on an apple he held in his left hand. His other hand reached out for mine. "Hi, Tom, call me Bill."

Within a few weeks, I had settled into a small, second-floor apartment on Main Street, two blocks from the office. The apartment, which I rented for $125 per month, consisted of an L-shaped living space with a makeshift bathroom to the left of the entryway and a bedroom to the right. The main living space was just big enough to host a yellow Formica table and two matching chairs. A small kitchen offered a gas stove, which I used to heat up canned ravioli, my meal of choice at the time. A refrigerator and sink accommodated the processed foods I ate and the dirty dishes I ignored for days on end. I positioned a mattress on the floor in the center of the bedroom. An assortment of cardboard boxes served as a dresser. I didn't have a television set or a stereo, and my AM radio was of limited use as it could receive only two stations in this valley between mountain ridges.

The *Enterprise* was an afternoon newspaper, which meant noon deadlines, printing around 1:30 and delivery by 3 p.m. As a one-man sports department, I had to fill those three pages. We had access to reams of copy from the Associated Press, which came in via the satellite dish connected to a teletype machine. Printed in blue ink on a continuous roll of paper, piled up in a heap at the base of the machine, the stories would be waiting for me every day. I walked down sloping Main Street each morning at 6 to be the first person in the office, cutting the teletype paper at the start of every new story. I'd stack them on my desk, noting which ones seemed as though they would be important to our readers. Bill left it up to me to decide what to run. How strange for a kid from the Midwest to be in charge of deciding what local New York fans would get to read.

Lake Placid attracted sports writers from national publications such as the *New York Times, Sports Illustrated* magazine, and *U.S. Today*. In town to cover a U.S. Olympic team trial, a *U.S. Today* writer suggested I send a resume to Gannett, the company that owned his newspaper and others all over the country. He said they'd probably have a place for me in a bigger market, which is what I thought I wanted – the opportunity to cover sports in ever-larger markets. I took his advice but when a couple months went by without word, I forgot about it.

* * *

Saranac Lake was very cold in the winter. The snow crunched under my feet as I walked to work in the predawn blackness. The still air felt like needles on the only skin I dared leave exposed – my nose, cheeks, and chin. Growing up in Minnesota, I knew what cold weather was all about but it felt even colder in Saranac Lake. Maybe it was because I was so far from family, living in a town where I made few friends. I didn't invite people to my apartment because it was too small to entertain. And I didn't have a car so my options for visiting others were limited, although Bill said I could sometimes use a company car.

A crusty man named Leo became my best friend. He lived alone two stories overhead in an apartment no larger than mine. He had a view out onto Main Street whereas my window looked out the back of the building. Leo had to be 80 years old, and he had the loose skin around his jaw and neck to prove it. We spent Thanksgiving together in 1983, a celebration that consisted of a TV dinner consumed in front of the television set that brought us a Detroit Lions football game. Leo smoked and the stale air of his living room was as thick as gravy. Leo must have shaved using one of those old-style manual razors because he had little cuts all over his face – short, clean, red incisions that were particularly striking on his chin and neck.

Leo was a talker and whatever I know about Saranac Lake, I learned from him. He had a distant relative who worked at the *Enterprise.*

"Do you know her?" he asked.

"Yes," I answered, since my desk was right next to hers.

Little more than an acquaintance, she covered city council meetings and local elections while I was covering basketball games and speed skating meets. With a child and no husband, she was trying to make a life for herself on a salary that couldn't have been much more than mine. Beyond our near-poverty-level incomes, we had little in common. I wondered why she wasn't spending Thanksgiving with Leo.

One day, I came home for lunch and found a brown paper bag at my door. Inside I found a clear plastic bag that held some kind of unidentifiable red carcass. Inching down the stairway behind me was Leo.

"It's for you," he said. "You can have it."

"What is it?"

"A rabbit."

He didn't tell me where it came from but he told me to be careful of buckshot.

"Thanks," I said.

I didn't know what to do with it; I had never eaten a rabbit before. When I was a little boy, the only stuffed animal that ever meant anything to me was a bunny. Later, my mother would tell me stories about working as a medical technologist in the 1950s when the standard pregnancy test involved injecting a rabbit with urine. After a few hours, they'd cut the rabbit open and make a determination according to the size of its internal organs. If the innards were swollen, the woman was pregnant. Mom said a large black woman on the hospital's cleaning staff used to take the dead rabbits home, where she would skin them and eat the meat. I put Leo's gift in the freezer.

After a few months, I worked up some courage, or maybe I grew tired of telling Leo I hadn't tried the rabbit yet. Nonetheless, I put the rabbit in an aluminum roasting pan I purchased at the Ben Franklin store, cranked up the oven and placed my meal on the cooking rack. I had no idea how to bake a rabbit but I figured it couldn't be all that different from a turkey, which I had seen my mother cook a number of times. Worried that the rabbit might have rabies or some other disease, I cooked the rabbit for hours. Totally overcooked, but certainly germ free, the rabbit came out of the oven dry as shoe leather. I sat down at my yellow dinner table and tried to carve the rabbit just like I had seen my father carve so many Thanksgiving Day turkeys. Considering its carbonized state, the meat wasn't bad, although it didn't taste like anything I had eaten before (not even chicken).

As I sat at the table, extracting BBs from the meat with knife and fork, I recalled a childhood neighbor, Mr. Bjallen, a man not unlike Leo. Mr. Bjallin and his wife lived in one of the smallest houses in the neighborhood where I grew up. In the summers, Mr. Bjallin would walk around the block in Bermuda shorts and an undershirt – a shirt cut like the ones weightlifters wear. He walked at a brisk pace, probably for his health, which looked to be suffering under his short, heavy stature. One day, he walked by while Peggy and I were playing basketball in the driveway and he asked if he could take a shot. We said sure. He grabbed the ball and walked up to the front of the driveway where he took a lay-up, falling backward to the ground as he let go of the ball. He lay horizontal on the pavement and began rolling down the driveway, making one revolution after another like a runaway log. We were certain he would roll into the busy street and be killed. But at the end of the driveway, he stopped and stood up, having regained his balance. He said he was fine, which is how I felt after eating Leo's rabbit; it went down okay with a couple of cans of Mountain Dew.

✳ ✳ ✳

Every Saturday during the fall I covered a high school football game, dividing the Tupper and Saranac schedules with Decker. (Lake Placid's high school didn't have a football team.) A high school football game in a small community, I learned, is a very important event – certainly more important than the football games I played in when I was a kid. Several hundred — perhaps more than a thousand — people came to watch the Saranac Lake Redskin and the Tupper Lake Lumberjack games we covered.

And before too long, I realized I was hopelessly ill-equipped to cover these games. As an outsider, I would never know as much about Northern Athletic League games as the locals who grew up with this brand of football as their primary form of entertainment. I would never understand what it meant to make the varsity, nor the way sixth and seventh graders worshipped the older boys on the team. I would never understand the parents, who called the players "men" and treated them like gods. Some got to miss class for practice; I was told they actually got an academic credit for being on the team. Parents treated them to elaborate spreads of food. The game day program featured pictures of each player. The games were broadcast live on the local radio station, and then rebroadcast later in the evening so the players could listen. We were expected to thoroughly cover the teams in the *Enterprise*.

A senior named John DeLay was a star player for the Redskins. During the season opener in 1983, he drew an unsportsmanlike conduct penalty that cost his team a first down. I described the situation in the story I wrote for the Monday edition of the *Enterprise*. Tuesday morning, John's dad stormed into the newspaper office.

"What do you put something like this in the paper for?" he barked.

"It was a key play," I said. "It affected the outcome of the game."

"You didn't have to report it!"

"I had to report what happened at the game."

"My boy has a chance to play college football. It's the only chance he has of getting to college. He'll never get a scholarship if you print stuff like this. He'll get a bad reputation."

Did Mr. DeLay really think his boy's reputation was in my hands? Couldn't Johnny just play by the rules? Maybe Mr. DeLay didn't think so, but I wasn't about to ask.

"Okay, I'll be more careful," I said and Mr. DeLay left the office.

Every time I saw Mr. DeLay after that I wondered about his kid's reputation.

❋ ❋ ❋

Saturday, October 1, 1983, Saranac Lake and Tupper Lake both had afternoon home games. Decker and I worked it out that I would go to the Lumber jacks' game in Tupper and he would cover the game in Saranac Lake. In the third game of the season, winless

Tupper Lake was playing the team from St. Lawrence, a squad that was struggling even more than the Lumberjacks. My parents happened to be in town that weekend, wanting to see how their budding reporter was doing after a few months on the job. We drove to the Tupper Lake field where Mom and Dad installed themselves behind the home team bench while I took a spot behind the visiting team's bench. I watched and listened carefully, keeping my own statistics and writing observations in a notebook. A rather uninteresting game unfolded, with the Tupper Lake team trouncing the Larries.

The coach for the St. Lawrence team, however, intrigued me with his coarse language. Several times when players came off the field after making a mistake, coach Jerry Mahoney greeted them with "get your head out of your ass!" I could hear him plain as day and I was sitting farther away from him than any of the fans sitting in the visitors' section of the bleachers. The coach's main form of communication was hollering and cursing — verbal abuse, clearly, and I couldn't believe that no one encouraged the coach to tone it down. The St. Lawrence Larries, were after all, high school kids who would not be allowed to watch a movie that featured such language.

Bob Tebo, who coached the Tupper Lake team, talked after the game about Mahoney's language.

"He was clearly frustrated," Bob said.

My parents talked about it on the return to

Saranac Lake.

"That coach has quite a mouth on him," Dad said.

"He sure does. I wanted to ask him about it but he wouldn't talk to me after the game," I said.

For Monday's *Enterprise,* I wrote: "Although the St. Lawrence Central players were the ones outscored on the field, Larries coach Jerry Mahoney showed himself to be the big loser." I described the game, including the verbal assaults by the coach. I explained that Mahoney gave spectators "a dark glimpse of high school football coaching." Most of the copy I generated ran in the newspaper without an editor's eye but I went out of my way to show this story to Bill Doolittle first. He loved it and applauded me for making a news story out of what otherwise would be just one more boring story about a high school football game. With Bill's approval, I knew I was on the right track. I even suggested a headline along the lines of ``Coach shows himself to be loser at football game" but Bill said we should go with something tamer. We ended up using: ``Tupper gets first win, beats St. Lawrence 31-7."

No readers wrote or called during the next few days to say anything about the story. Following the Mr. DeLay incident, I half expect the coach's mother to come in and chew me out.

But apparently, it was too soon to assume everything was okay. The Friday following the Thanksgiving I celebrated with Leo, a uniformed state trooper came into the *Enterprise* office. He asked for me.

"What's this?" I asked as he handed me an envelope.

"You didn't know about this?" he asked.

"No."

The envelope contained a summons addressed to the newspaper and me. Jerry Mahoney was suing us for defamation, seeking $200,000 in compensatory damages and another $200,000 in punitive damages. I couldn't believe it! Mahoney charged in the suit that I got the story all wrong. He claimed I made up the foul language.

If this was how Mahoney felt, I wondered aloud, why didn't he talk to me after the story ran? We would have run his side of the story or a clarification. We hadn't heard a word from him, so the summons hit me like a ton of bricks.

"What are we going to do?" I asked Bill.

"Don't worry about it," Bill said. "These kinds of things happen all the time. The newspaper will hire the best lawyer around and the suit will probably be thrown out long before it gets to court."

But I couldn't help but worry. Was I wrong to write about the coach's behavior? Did I really defame him? What if we lost the lawsuit? Would I owe Mahoney $400,000? How would I pay him?

Ogden Newspapers, the Wheeling, West Virginia, company that owned the *Enterprise*, hired Henry Fisher to defend us. He had an unflappable demeanor that boosted our confidence. He had been involved in similar cases and he assured us he knew what to do. Bill was convinced 'we should try to scare the heck out of Mahoney by calling in everyone at the game for a deposition. "We should call in his mother and ask her if he swore when he was a boy," Bill said. The situation was bringing out a side of Bill that Decker had told me about — the Bill whose first job in journalism was working for one of the New York City daily tabloids. He had to visit the family homes of murder and accident victims, and acquire pictures of them off a mantel or bedside stand so the newspaper could publish them. Bill put on a refined exterior as publisher of the *Enterprise* but at his core I could see how scrappy he was. He would do whatever it took to survive.

Fisher, however, took a low-key approach. The only depositions he took were from Bill and me. He didn't even ask the court for a change of venue, which Bill and I thought would be important. We were being sued in St. Lawrence County, where the coach lived. There, we were convinced, he would get a jury of his buddies and we'd have no chance for a fair trial. We thought it would be better to try the case in Franklin County, which included Tupper Lake. Fisher, nonetheless, wasn't worried.

* * *

The courtroom at the St. Lawrence County City Hall was large and looked exactly like the courtrooms in every episode of *Perry Mason* I had ever seen. Bill and I wore suits and ties, while Mohoney wore casual pants and a golf shirt. My attire set me up for the attack they took, which was that I was a know-it-all kid from the big city with a bias against people from small communities. They also tried to demonstrate that being inexperienced and poorly trained, I never should have been assigned to cover the game.

"Are you a member of Sigma Delta Chi or any other professional journalism fraternal organizations?" Mahoney's attorney asked me on the stand.

"No."

"Have you ever won any journalism awards or been recognized by your peers for outstanding work?" he asked.

"No," I answered, looking at the faces of the 12 people sitting in the jury box.

"Prior to your job at the *Enterprise*, had you ever worked at a newspaper as a professional journalist?"

"No."

Then he asked me about details of the game, which I found impossible to remember. It had taken more than two years to bring the case to trial.

"How many coaches were assisting the head coach?"

"I have no idea."

"Were you at the game?

"Of course."

"Then tell us how many coaches assisted the head coach."

"Two or three," I guessed.

"Which is it? Two or three?" he persisted.

"Two," I said to shut him up.

"How many interceptions did the Larries quarterback throw that afternoon?"

"I have no idea."

"In your article of October 3, 1983, you say he was intercepted six times."

"Then it was six times," I said.

The attorney later told the jury that Mahoney had only one assistant. He also said the official scorebook for the game indicated the Larries recorded four interceptions. He was painting me as someone who really didn't care about what I was writing, and didn't care who I might be hurting in the process. As I listened I wanted to go back on the stand and explain to the jury that the official scorebook was often wrong. The statistics generally were recorded by a kid who wasn't smart enough to make the football team. I didn't trust those stats and that's why I kept my own. Henry Fisher then got his chance to call witnesses and address the jury.

"Did you holler at your players?" Fisher asked Mahoney.

"No. I mean, not any more than usual," he answered.

"Did you not say to them on the day in question 'get your head out of your ass?' " Fisher asked.

"No" he answered.

I couldn't believe it. This man was committing perjury!

"Did you say anything like that?" Fisher persisted.

"I said 'get your head up,' " the coach answered. "I always tell the kids to carry their heads high with pride, no matter how the game is going. I told the kids to keep their head up."

At that point I knew I was dead. With him claiming to say something different than what I heard, it came down to my word against his, and the jury was going to believe him a lot more readily than it was going to believe me. But Fisher remained confident. He told Bill and me that a high school football coach in a small town is a public official, kind of like the mayor or the governor. It is almost impossible for a public official to win a defamation case. People have a right to comment on public officials, Fisher said. Furthermore, Fisher said Mahoney had not demonstrated that he suffered in any way as a result of the article I wrote. In order to win damages in a defamation suit, the plaintiff must demonstrate that he suffered a true loss, such as being fired or being denied a promotion. Nothing like that happened to Mahoney. Fisher explained all of this to the jury in a closing argument.

The jury left the room to deliberate. Bill and I waited around for several minutes when I excused myself to use the restroom. As I relieved myself, I thought about my situation. Was I pissing away my whole life with small-time journalism? Did 12 jurors, two attorneys, a judge, a bailiff, and a court reporter really have nothing better to do than listen to a foul-mouth football coach lie about the way he treats his players? I couldn't believe I was somehow caught up in the middle of all this. As I adjusted the faucet on the sink, I thought about how I wanted to wash my hands of the whole thing.

Upon returning to the courtroom, I found Bill putting on his coat. The jury had returned and announced a guilty verdict while I was in the men's room! I couldn't believe it. The only time in my life I had ever been involved in a lawsuit and the verdict is announced while I'm in the bathroom?! I was livid. Bill was in no mood to talk. We got into his car and drove back to Saranac Lake in deadly silence.

All the way back I thought to myself how Fisher had screwed up. Why hadn't he called more witnesses? Maybe Bill was right, we should have gotten depositions from everyone at the game. Then, at least, it would not have simply been my word against the coach's. Plenty of people heard the coach use exactly the same language I reported in my story. Why didn't we call in my parents? They heard the coach swear. Or how about Bob Tebo, the Tupper Lake coach? Why didn't we call him to the witness stand? We missed every opportunity we had but Fisher still told us not to worry. I had a hard time believing him now. This was the biggest problem I ever faced in my life and I trusted it to a stranger. What a mistake. Bill and I should have handled this on our own. We knew what to do. Fisher clearly did not.

But we left it in Fisher's hands. He said we would appeal to a higher court where the judge was more likely to give us a fair trial. Although we wouldn't be able to enter new evidence into the case, we also wouldn't have to worry about a jury full of cronies.

News of our defeat preceded us to Saranac Lake. Even the Saranac Lake High School football coach had heard the outcome already. I ran into him as I walked up Main Street in front of the *Enterprise* office.

"I can't believe Mahoney won that suit," he said to me. "You know, we coaches were all sitting around playing cards one night shortly after you wrote that story. We told Mahoney he ought to sue the bastards! Damn, if he didn't do it and win."

3

Home

I moved out East to get a job but really I was looking for a home, a place to make the life that I thought I wanted. Within two years, I knew I needed to return to the Midwest. Upstate New York was beautiful but my heritage wasn't there. Nor were my lifelong friends and family. I missed the things I had as a kid – familiar surroundings, common experiences with my neighbors, and the comfort of knowing I belonged. I returned to Minneapolis, ultimately discovering that home was the place where I grew up.

My path, however, wasn't straight; I tacked, stopping in Binghamton, New York, for about a year. I had been with the *Enterprise* for only eight months when Gannett responded to the letter I'd sent. They had an opening at the Binghamton *Press Sun Bulletin*, a newspaper whose name revealed a past checkered with mergers. With editions published in the morning and early evening, *Press Sun Bulletin* writers were required to produce several versions of every story they wrote, a great exercise for a budding writer, I was told. I took the job, figuring I could learn a lot from the other 12 people on the sports staff.

Tom Borrelli, a short, round man with a flattop haircut, was hired the same day I was. The first day on the job, each of us was assigned a simple story to write for the next day's edition. I proceeded at my usual pace, checking facts, looking up names, and consulting the dictionary as I committed my words to the newspaper's central work-processing system, which we accessed through computer terminals at our desks. I was just beginning to record my first words when Borrelli asked for his next assignment. He was done! I had never seen anyone write so quickly. "His story must be full of mistakes," I thought, but then an editor who had already finished reading the story hollered over, "Nice job, Borrelli."

Borrelli was dubbed "Ox" by the rest of the staff, perhaps to eliminate confusion that could result over us sharing the same first name. It wasn't "The Ox," or "Mr. Ox," just Ox, which seemed to match his stark personality. Borrelli kind of liked the name because it played up his brute strength, evidenced by biceps that were as thick as my thighs. A weightlifter, he invited me to his efficiency apartment once to show me his dumbbells and weights, which occupied most of his living space.

The bread and butter of the *Press Sun Bulletin* sports section was coverage of the various high school teams. Most of the stories I wrote revolved around scholastic cross-country meets, swim competitions, and football games. My most glamorous ongoing assignment was backup on the minor league hockey beat. The Binghamton Whalers were an American Hockey League affiliate of the NHL's Hartford Whalers and I got to cover games when the lead reporter on the beat wasn't available. I had watched a lot of hockey games as a kid, even played a little at the Park Board level. The opportunity to get up close to a professional hockey team and interview players intrigued me. At least initially.

"What do you do besides play hockey?" I asked an up-and-coming player after a practice.

"Chase pussy," he said.

"Excuse me?"

"You know, women," he clarified.

"Anything else?"

"Is there anything else?" he asked.

"Are a lot of women interested in hockey?" I asked.

"There are always girls who want to meet players after games," he said. "We party and have a good time."

Long, silent pause as I turned the pages of my notebook, desperately trying to think of something worthwhile to ask.

"What kinds of things did you do in high school?"

"I played a lot of hockey," he responded. "Do you want my autograph?"

I declined.

I never got to know any of the players much more than that, and the appeal associated with writing about them wore off quickly. After a few months on the job, I could see that the work at the *Press Sun Bulletin* was a lot like the work at the *Enterprise*, only worse without the intermittent opportunities to cover the U.S. Olympic team, world-class skiers, or internationally known figure skaters. Sure, I was paid a little more now and many more people were seeing my work, but the trade-off proved unsatisfying.

The closer I got to big-time sports, the more I could see it wasn't anything at all like the experiences I had as a kid, when sports seemed like something really special. My dad, for example, started taking me to Gopher football games when I turned 8 years old. A day at the game was a big deal. We'd arrive well ahead of the 1:30 kickoff so we'd have sufficient time to make the mile-and-a-half hike to the stadium from the free parking we took near the abandoned railroad tracks. Our early start also got us to the main gates of the massive brick stadium in time to see the University of Minnesota Golden Gopher marching band parade down 4th Street and into the bowl end of the U-shaped arena. I revered the marching students like super-heroes. The gold stripe down the side of each maroon pant leg and the tall hat with the plume in front made band members seem larger than life. Even in the cool fall weather, I could see the sweat dripping off the faces of many of the marchers. They lifted their knees, turned at their waists, and bobbed their heads in ways that I never seemed to be able to imitate.

Our seats, midway up the bowl section of the stadium, offered only a distant view of the game. Dad said it was the perfect perch for "watching the plays unfold," a line that I bought well into my teens. As a kid who was happy to spend an afternoon with my dad, the seats seemed great; I could see everything I wanted to see. Straight ahead was the scoreboard that sat on the roof of Cooke Hall. To my right was the student section where every now and then fans in the lower rows would pick up a college girl and pass her overhead to the people in the higher rows. Fans along the way generally cooperated, keeping the process going until the girl reached the very top row. I always watched to see what they would do next, but they never tossed her over. To my left was the quieter side of the stadium, where alumni and visiting fans sat.

My dad had been a Gopher football fan since he was a kid, listening to games on radio from his home on Grand Avenue in south Minneapolis. He tells me he used to diagram the plays as they were described over the airwaves. Once he showed me a scrapbook he assembled with all his game charts, each drawn with the precision of a draftsman. Dad says he used to read the peach-colored sports section of the Sunday newspaper and cut out stories about the big games, saving them in another scrapbook he kept. He showed me that one too.

Maybe I was trying to connect with my father by becoming a sports writer. As I stumbled along my career path, I began to realize that it wasn't the sport that held the magic, it was my dad. The camaraderie, companionship, and friendship I got from family as a kid were simply missing from my life in upstate New York. Ox, Cheese, Jaws, and the other *Press Sun Bulletin* sports writers with funny nicknames were friendly enough, but they never became like the family I so desperately needed to feel at home.

* * *

My colleagues quickly picked up on my Midwest congeniality and Ox dubbed me "Opie." Furthermore, my easygoing personality made me an obvious target for pranks at the office. For example, when I would use a stall in the men's room, Ox would come into the bathroom after me, pick up a bar of soap from one of the sinks and throw it as hard as he could at the stall door. Bam! The first time he did it I thought a bomb had gone off. He repeated this prank many times, despite my requests for a little peace and quiet. I eventually became so disconcerted by these "soapings" that I stopped using the restroom, which made me a lot less comfortable at my desk.

Another time, Ox told me a news anchor from ESPN had called. Ox said the guy wanted to talk to me about some of the work I did in Lake Placid. I fell for it hook, line, and sinker. Ox provided a phone number, I called, and Mr. ESPN answered. When I identified myself as the person he had called earlier, he responded "I didn't call you." My mouth dropped, I hung up the phone and lifted my head to see my colleagues hunched over with laughter.

I was no stranger to practical jokes but I wasn't used to being the punch line time and time again. In grade school, my buddies and I played all kinds of tricks. But we were kids, not adults, and I almost always felt a little guilt about tricking anyone. One winter Sunday afternoon, my friend Mark Hillendbrand and I were itching to play tennis. We came up with the idea of playing in the gymnasium of Resurrection Grade School. So we walked over to the convent across the street to talk to the principal. Amazingly, she handed us a set of keys. We went over to the school and played but grew bored after about a half an hour, so with a loaded key ring in hand, we decided to take a look around the school.

We went to our homeroom and unlocked the door. We found a piece of chalk. In huge letters, we wrote a vulgar word on the blackboard. First I wrote an "F," then a "U." By the time I completed the word with the last two letters, the vulgarity filled the entire blackboard. We used the side of the chalk to make the letters extra thick. We thought it would be hilarious when the teacher came to school the following morning, opened the classroom door and found this word on her blackboard. She would have to ask any kids she was with to wait in the hallway while she erased it. Ha, ha, ha. What a great prank!

After locking the door, returning the keys and retreating to Mark's bedroom, we laughed about what we had done. But then we grew silent. A feeling of guilt grew in us, or maybe it was just fear. Surely they would figure out who did it and we would be in trouble. So we walked back to the convent. The principal answered the door. We told her we forgot some tennis balls in the gym. Could we borrow her keys again? Thankfully, she handed us the keys without question. We ran over to the school, went to the classroom, and erased what we had written on the blackboard. The chalk was so heavy, however, that we ended up having to wash the blackboard. Then with the one blackboard washed, it was much brighter than the other two in the room. We decided the clean blackboard would look conspicuous so we washed the other blackboards as well. By the time we left, the room was much cleaner than it was before we arrived. We returned the keys to Sister and felt a whole lot better.

I never got the feeling that Ox and the other pranksters at the *Press Sun Bulletin* felt any guilt. One Saturday morning I came into the office and checked my mailbox. The high school football season was opening and I was checking in before heading out to a game. An official-looking memo was stuffed into my mailbox, along with a wadded up *Press Sun Bulletin* T-shirt. The memo explained that all reporters were required to wear the company T-shirt at events we covered. So I put it on and went to cover the game. Four hours later when I returned to the office, the sports section of the newsroom was a-buzz with reporters who had covered other games. When they looked up to see me coming in with my T-shirt on, they broke out in laughter. Ox had written the fake memo and I looked like an idiot. The *Press Sun Bulletin* wasn't the home I was looking for.

The more I thought about my situation at the *Press Sun Bulletin*, the more I wanted to go back to Minneapolis. The sports editor who hired me got promoted soon after I joined the newspaper and I never saw him again. I ended up working for another guy who told me that if it were up to him he never would have hired me. Ox, who was hired by the same editor who was promoted, kept telling me to hang in there. He thought the *Press Sun Bulletin* was a great place to work. But the more he encouraged me, the more I realized I had to leave. What was I staying for? It certainly wasn't the money. I figured I could stay in Binghamton and be poor and be more than 1,000 miles from my friends and family, or I could move back to Minneapolis and be poor and at least be near my friends and family.

* * *

Taking up residence with my parents in my old room, I set out on a job search in the Twin Cities. After four months of searching in a recessionary economy, I landed a reporting job with a trade magazine. *Commercial West* covered the banking industry in an eight-state region that was home to some 2,000 banks — mostly small, family-run institutions. Although I was initially unsure about making the transition from the sports desk to the business beat, it turned out that covering banking wasn't all that different. Instead of the Syracuse Orangemen, I had to know First Bank System. Instead of understanding batting averages, I had to learn about return on equity. I found I liked the world of banking. Most bankers were very nice to me, which I didn't expect given the many negative things I had heard about bankers from acquaintances who were quick to tell me about some bad experience they had had with a bounced check, ill-functioning automatic teller machine, or denied loan application.

The industry, I quickly learned, was going through tremendous changes that provided fodder for stories more engaging than any football game or track meet. In 1980, the law opened up the banking industry to competition it had never known before. No longer would Uncle Sam tell banks what they could pay on checking and savings accounts. For the first time, bankers could pay whatever they wanted to attract deposits and charge whatever they wanted to make a loan.

As it turned out, the 1980s proved to be a funny time to deregulate banking. Inflation was at an all-time high in the early part of the decade. While the Midwest suffered from an agricultural crisis, other parts of the country were suffering from a real estate bust and problems in the oil economy. And the biggest banks got into a mess lending to Third World countries. By the time I started covering the industry in 1985, banking was in real trouble. As many as 200 banks a year were failing and the rest were struggling to adapt to the deregulated environment. Competition from mutual fund companies was forcing bankers to get out and sell their services for the first time in history. It was a difficult transition for people in three-piece suits who made careers out of sitting behind their desks, waiting for customers to come to them.

Through countless conversations, I learned first-hand of the turmoil. Many of the banks in the *Commercial West* coverage area specialized in lending to farmers who needed loans to pay for seed, fertilizer, and other necessities of spring planting. When the harvest came in, farmers were supposed to be able to sell their crops for enough money to pay off the loans and have a little left over for themselves. In the 1980s, the cost of planting often exceeded what the farmer could get for his yield in the fall. This meant that a lot of the bankers who lent money to those farmers had trouble collecting repayment. And in some areas, the price of farmland was soaring. Farmers would borrow from the bank to acquire land, and then fail to generate enough income from that land to even cover the interest payments on the loan. This caused incredible stress for bankers and farmers. Major newspapers were reporting the farmers' stories but I was the only one covering bankers.

Writing about the farm crisis was relatively easy from the confines of my office, which was 20 miles from the nearest farm. Advocacy groups active in Washington, D.C., were always willing to give interviews and feed me the latest research on the dire nature of the farmer's plight. And banker groups – the American Bankers Association and the Independent Community Bankers of America – gave me the story from the banker's perspective. I would attend industry meetings, notebook and camera in hand, where I would listen to the experts tell bankers they had to be ready to write off millions of dollars in debt to farmers who were never going to make it.

My favorite thing to do was to visit a farm, which usually reminded me of my grandparents' farm in central Minnesota. Czechoslovakian immigrants who barely paused from farming to raise my mother and her sister, Grandpa and Grandma Danko eked out a sparse living. Their tiny house lacked even the simplest amenities – running water, electricity, a telephone. But Mom said Grandpa loved that farm. For Grandpa, agriculture was the future, his ticket to riches. My mother said she remembers her dad standing in the middle of his living room, declaring "I never thought I'd have all this."

Visiting farms for *Commercial West*, I never found

that level of enthusiasm. One farmer pointed to a row of cows that he milked twice a day, every day, for years, and complained that he could barely get enough money for the milk to make it worth feeding the cows. Another farmer boasted about getting 180 bushels of corn from an acre of land – probably the highest yield in the world – but he said it still wasn't enough to cover his costs. Most farmers were seeking employment off the farm to supplement their income but jobs in small towns were hard to come by. All of this was news to me, and I wrote about it like it was news to my readers. But they knew far better than I did what was really going on. The ag bankers, as we called them at the magazine, could see the country transforming into an information-based society away from the agrarian culture that it had been in the first half of the 20th century. The story was so much bigger than anything I could ever fully understand, but the snippets I got to cover fascinated me.

Robert Hadland, for example, showed me what it was like to be a small town ag banker in the mid-1980s. Hadland was president of the Farmers & Merchants State Bank in Lamberton, a southwest Minnesota town with a population of just more than 1,000 people. Hadland had left a job with the American Lutheran Church in Minneapolis in 1977 to buy the tiny financial institution. In December of 1985, I visited him to do a story on unique efforts he was taking to save his troubled bank. About a third of the bank's loans were in trouble, according to reports from regulators, and if he didn't turn things around in a hurry, they were going to close the bank. Needing about $2 million to shore things up, Hadland called a meeting at the town's American Legion Hall, where he announced a public stock offering. The idea was so unique that CBS and the *Wall Street Journal* followed up with stories. So did *Commercial West*.

Hadland spent an afternoon with me, explaining how difficult things were. Had he sold the bank two years earlier, Hadland said, he could have walked away with $2 million in his pocket. Now he would be lucky to get out of town without filing for bankruptcy. His problems, he told me, were related to the farm situation, which was dire in southwestern Minnesota.

Hadland cited an example where in January 1984 a customer's farm machinery was valued at $94,000. Fourteen months later, when the farmer began to have trouble repaying loans to the bank, Hadland encouraged him to liquidate. An auctioneer assessed the value of the same machinery at $52,000. By the time the machinery was sold "we were lucky to get $30,000 out of it," Hadland said.

A typical $20 million bank like the Farmers & Merchants should generate about $150,000 in net income every year while paying the president a near-six-figure salary. But Hadland's bank was far from typical. He told me he cut his salary in half to $40,000 and gave up a lot of perks – things like a boat on Lake Superior, an antique automobile, and season tickets to the Minnesota Orchestra. He and his wife had just built a big house. Five years earlier, when times were good, it made sense to spend $240,000 to build a home in Lamberton; now it was only a reminder of an investment they'd never be able to recoup. I felt sorry for this 61-year-old man, even though I knew there may have been poor business decisions made along the way. I knew that a man in his 60s who had worked hard all his life should be able to look forward to a comfortable retirement. A 40-year-old man who files for bankruptcy could always start his life over; a 60-year-old man wouldn't really have that option.

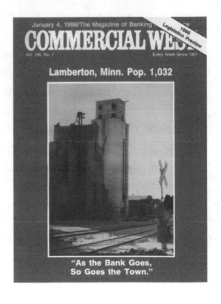

January 4, 1986/The Magazine of Banking

COMMERCIAL WEST

Vol. 109, No. 1

Every Week Since 1901

Legislative Preview 1986

Lamberton, Minn. Pop. 1,032

"As the Bank Goes, So Goes the Town."

I took several photos of Lamberton and the bank. I took pictures of Hadland at his desk, in the lobby, and at a teller window. As I focused the camera to capture one pose, Hadland began to cry. He had just spent the last 45 minutes telling me about his life. The tears made me nervous and I couldn't think of anything to say. Finally, I just said "smile" and snapped a couple of photos. A stark picture I·took of the town's grain elevator ran on the cover of the January 4, 1986, edition of *Commercial West*. The art director chose to run the photo under a blue tint, which gave the wintry picture a particularly lonely look. Hadland eventually lost his bank, as did more than 1,000 other bankers in the 1980s.

But whether it was Hadland or someone else, I loved it when a banker in a small community would invite me to visit with him at a local café. I was always struck by how ordinary bankers were despite the power they held over the financial future of those around them. Consider that the typical community banker decides whom to lend money to, and whom to deny. A banker decides which farmers stay in business and which ones have to seek new lines of work. The banker decides which businesses will come to town and which will go elsewhere. Usually, he is a key player in community decisions about hospital expansions, industrial park construction, real estate development, school initiatives, and other efforts that affect the identity of a town.

It sounds like a great life but, similar to the prince who is cloistered in his own castle, I could see that power sometimes brings loneliness, and I knew from my Binghamton days how troubling loneliness could be. Imagine going to church Sunday morning and taking a pew behind the man whose loan you denied a few days earlier. What would it be like to sit in a restaurant, knowing the financial details of most of the customers around you? *That one is on the verge of bankruptcy; that guy just bought a house that will stretch him to the limit; the man over there has no retirement savings; and the one next to him just collected a small inheritance.* Discretion is perhaps the banker's best friend.

After I interviewed the president of a bank in a community of 250 people, he invited me to his home for coffee and apple pie. I got in my car, which was parked on Main Street in front of the bank, and followed him four blocks to his home, a modest rambler with an attached double garage. We sat in the dining room where his wife served us pie she had made that morning. The hospitality seemed genuine and, like the pie, was warm. Sometimes I couldn't believe I was a reporter. Weren't reporters supposed to be digging through police records or looking for contraband in the city's warehouse district? Weren't people usually shooing reporters out of their offices? That was only in the movies or maybe at other publications.

As a writer, I found my home at *Commercial West*. I took comfort in the trade journal format, writing stories about things that worked well, about interesting people, and about everyday challenges in an evolving industry. After some time on the job, I began to fantasize about owning the magazine, running it well into my old age, kind of like the newspaper editor in Thornton Wilder's play, *Our Town*.

Emerging Son

With my employment situation firmed up, I felt ready to move out of my parent's house. I found a roomy apartment near Lake Calhoun. Setting up a desk with a computer in my bedroom, I spent many evenings typing my thoughts onto five-and-a-quarter-inch floppy disks. I recalled my last day at the Binghamton *Press Sun Bulletin*. Throughout my year there, I kidded Ox about beating him at arm wrestling. Ox was strong but I surmised he looked stronger than he was. Since my arm was longer than his, I knew I would have a leverage advantage. Ox always blew off my challenges but on my last day at the newspaper the other guys in the sports department wouldn't let him dismiss me. "Give him a chance," the guys said to Ox. So we cleared off a desk in the middle of the sports department and locked wrists. People from other departments joined the sports staff to watch the impromptu match. People cheered as Ox and I pushed against each other with all our strength. Ox's face turned red. A vein emerged from his forehead. Our arms shook. Minutes seemed to pass. Finally, I slammed his wrist to the table! Nobody could believe it, but I won.

More than a year later, I was beginning to believe that I really had won. Surrounded by friends and family, magazine writing seemed a lot more homey to me than newspaper reporting with irreverent colleagues back East.

Writing in my apartment one evening, I got a call from my old boss at the *Adirondack Daily Enterprise*,

Bill Doolittle. He told me that the lawsuit involving the St. Lawrence football coach cleared up in our favor. The New York Court of Appeals overturned the jury verdict and a subsequent appellate division order against the *Enterprise* and me. The court said that because the plaintiff was a public figure, the law required him to prove the article was published with "actual malice." This meant he would have had to prove that I deliberately set out to hurt his reputation. Of course I did not, so the plaintiff couldn't prove it. My article was not malicious and, in fact, the whole mess could have been avoided if Mahoney had talked to me after that football game on October 1, 1983.

The Associated Press picked up on the court's decision and ran a story about it that appeared in many newspapers. The story didn't do much for my ego but it did even less for Jerry Mahoney. I was painted as a sloppy cub reporter but he came off a loser, much the same as in the story I wrote. The suit had left me tentative and unsure, but successful resolution of the case now gave me a new sense of confidence.

4

Pilgrimage

Working for newspapers and a magazine, I learned that journalism is the process of identifying and describing conflict. I wrote hundreds of stories about people competing against one another, or about groups lined up on opposite sides of an issue. Even the lighthearted stories I wrote usually featured someone working against the odds. I found that just as it was impossible to race a sailboat without thinking about the America's Cup, it was impossible to write stories without contemplating the ultimate conflict — good versus evil.

People who read *Commercial West* knew what I considered to be good and evil. Bankers in community-based institutions were good, while greedy investors, over-reaching regulators, and scam artists were evil. Creators, hard-workers, and entrepreneurs were good while lazy pessimists and self-serving politicians were evil. Even when I covered sports, I naturally viewed the newspaper's hometown team as the good guys and the other team as the bad guys. Their very uniforms (light versus dark) encouraged this kind of thinking. It was a code I'd learned as a kid watching Westerns on television where everyone feared the gunman in the black hat.

In some stories, however, it was not so clear who was the good guy and who was bad. People didn't wear telltale uniforms in the real world. Although conflicts were obvious in business, banking, and politics, it wasn't always apparent which side represented good and which side represented evil. I struggled for answers; sometimes they never came.

Good and evil are concepts I had been thinking about since before I would write. I wanted to know what distinguished one from the other. I assumed it mattered, but did it? What do I need to do to be truly happy? And what about death – what will happen after that? Reporters are supposed to ask tough questions, and I guess I got started early. One impromptu theological discussion at the dinner table gave me a chance to reveal the fruits of my contemplation.

"Dad, how can you prove God exists?" asked Terri, whose teacher had posed the question to sixth-graders earlier that day.

I didn't wait for Dad to answer. With a mouth full of potatoes, I answered for him. "Who do you think makes your heart beat?"

"What do you mean?" my sister asked.

"Why does your heart beat inside of you but not inside of a dead person?" I pursued. "God is the only answer. If God doesn't exist, then how do you explain your heart beating?"

Terri didn't have an answer. Neither did my dad.

＊　＊　＊

Upon my return to Minneapolis, I looked up an old college buddy. Jim Johnson was a reporter at the University of Minnesota's student *Daily* when I was the newspaper's sports editor. He grew up in a working class section of Bloomington, was friendly, and smiled a lot, which made him unique at the *Daily* where cynicism was in vogue. Jim could write any kind of story but his strength was the personality profile. If he was assigned to write a feature about a hockey player, a gymnast, or a volleyball player, he'd come back with prose that would make the sports section sing. He could capture an individual's personality and express it in words as well as any journalist with decades of experience.

I cut Jim some slack when he told me he wouldn't work on Sundays. At the *Daily*, a five-day-a-week newspaper, sportswriters almost always worked on Sundays. The big games took place on Fridays or Saturdays, so most writers came into the office on Sunday afternoon to polish their stories before turning them in for the Sunday evening deadline. Jim said he would get all his work done by Saturday night. Sometimes there would be a development on Sunday that would affect the stories but I didn't push him too hard on the issue. His copy was usually clean enough that by the time I looked at it, there were few editing changes to be made.

During the intervening years, Jim had landed an internship with the Gannett-owned Des Moines *Register*. The internship was considered a stepping-stone to a permanent job at a daily newspaper in a major market. I hadn't secured my job at *Commercial West* yet, and I was curious about what it was like to work at a Pulitzer-prize winning newspaper, so I visited Jim in early July 1985. Without air conditioning, it must have been 100 degrees in my car during the 240-mile ride to Des Moines. Driving with the windows open, the hot air swirled around making it impossible to keep any loose papers, like a map, on the seat next to me. The McDonald's wrappers generally discarded on the floor behind the front seats flew out the window somewhere around Owatonna.

I arrived in Des Moines near quitting time. I was soaked in sweat as I wandered into the newsroom, which looked a lot like the newsroom at the Binghamton *Press Sun Bulletin*. Jim was seated at a neatly arranged desk in a cubical and although he was expecting me, he acted surprised when I showed up. High-fiving and laughing, we greeted each other with slaps on the back.

We spent the weekend together, mostly catching

up on the last two years. He told me he loved journalism but he didn't like some of the stupid stories he was asked to write. Once, for example, the newspaper was writing a series of stories on a stadium proposal. Jim's assignment was to look at the blueprints and determine whether the stadium would have sufficient toilet facilities. His editor made him call major league stadium managers all over the country to ask for a breakdown on the number of their men's and women's restrooms. Apparently the numbers weren't automatically the same.

Jim and I went to an Iowa Cubs baseball game on Saturday night. Triple-A ball in an outdoor ballpark was a real treat to a sports fan who typically watched home baseball games under a cavernous plastic dome. I was like many baseball fans in Minnesota who longed for the old days when the Twins played outdoors. Jim, who had sold hot dogs at Bloomington's old Metropolitan Stadium when he was in high school, shared my sentiments. Sec Taylor stadium in downtown Des Moines was both a haven and a comforting reminder of our youth.

We met a friend at the ballpark, a woman who obviously had eyes for Jim. After enjoying the game, the gal asked Jim if we wanted to meet her for dancing at a local drinking establishment. I was astonished when he said no.

That night, in his living room where I was sleeping on the floor, Jim sat back in a chair, clasped his hands behind his head and stretched his legs. He looked relaxed and in a mood to talk, despite the late hour. I asked him why he refused the invitation from the comely young woman. He told me he couldn't go into a place like that because of his "commitment to God." I had no idea what he was talking about. He elaborated, telling me he had committed his life to Christ. Describing his faith in dramatic terms, Jim talked about being "saved" and he said he lived with the assurance that comes with knowing he will spend eternity in paradise. He talked about the Bible, quoting verses with fluency. Then he asked me about my faith; I couldn't think of anything to say. My story about proving God's existence with a heartbeat no longer seemed profound.

Driving back to Minneapolis, I thought a lot about what Jim said. His conviction spoke volumes. And I couldn't deny he lived with a light heart; he obviously had something going for him that few of my peers did. As the road signs marked my advancement toward the Twin Cities – Ames, Jewell, Clear Lake, Manly, and Albert Lea – I thought about my own childhood experiences with religion.

Resurrection Church was only a block from our house so we walked to Sunday morning Mass, which was at 7:30, 9:00, 10:30, and noon, the ample schedule indicating an abundance of priests and believers in the 1960s. When I was very young, Mass included prayers in Latin and we used to kneel to receive communion.

Later, I remember the day they introduced the "sign of peace" into the liturgy. Ushers walked to the front of the church to shake the hand of the person sitting at the end of each pew. They worked their way toward the back of the church, encouraging parishioners to follow suit and shake the hand of their neighbor. No one knew what to make of this liturgical reform that had come out of the great series of meetings known as the Second Vatican Council. Many Resurrection parishioners regarded the handshake as a fad; certainly it wouldn't last.

My father had been an altar boy at Incarnation Parish in Minneapolis and I followed in his footsteps, taking up the role of acolyte at Resurrection. His job was a lot harder than mine because he had to memorize several prayers in Latin; by the time I became an altar boy in 1972, no one was saying prayers in Latin anymore. I only had to remember where to go, where to stand, and when to bring things to the priest during Mass. My biggest worry was tripping over the hem of my cassock, which never seemed to fit quite right. I was so nervous before the very first Mass I served that Fr. Huff could see my hands shaking. He said a prayer over me to calm my nerves.

I liked being an altar boy, which gave me access to the sacristy, that room behind the altar that served as a meeting place for our "secret society." Altar boys got to light candles and play with incense. We were in charge of the sound system that was secured behind a locked cabinet. Holy relics were everywhere, things such as the chalice and ciborium, which we could touch only under special circumstances. One time, I dropped a chalice and the Monsignor looked at me with such horror that I thought I was going to die on the spot. Never saying a word, he picked it up and I lived.

We were supposed to genuflect and cross ourselves every time we passed in front of a crucifix. And, of course, there was the wine. We had to pour a little of the red liquid into a cruet before Mass. After removing the screw-on cap, I poured the wine and smelled it, mostly out of curiosity, which never diminished even after serving hundreds of Masses. The aroma was sweet. I wanted to taste it but I never did. Older boys warned us that servers who consumed the wine were banned from altar boy service for the rest of their lives. I always assumed they were taken to the basement through one of the doors in the sacristy that was always locked, and punished in some painful, yet holy, way. Girls weren't allowed to be acolytes. For me, this made serving Mass better than studying in school, where girls distracted me.

Few altar boys would engage the priest in conversation, but I would.

"Gonna watch the Viking's game this afternoon?" I asked the Monsignor.

"Oh, Thomas," he said, "I don't have time for football."

"What kinds of things do you have time for?"

"I do a lot of reading. Plus, running a parish takes a lot of time," he said. "Oh look, it's time to start Mass."

I enjoyed the special services, like Stations of the Cross and Easter Vigil. Myths, perpetuated by the older altar boys, evolved about how we were to serve. For example, I was told that during Stations of the Cross, the cross bearer was not allowed to rest the cross on the ground at each station. This was absurd but I believed it and would try to keep the large, heavy cross elevated during the entire 45-minute service. Every muscle in my arms and shoulders were shaking by the fourth station.

Easter Vigil, taking place late on the Saturday before Easter, was the granddaddy of all Masses. Every altar boy in the parish participated. The Mass opened with a procession that seemed to take forever as more and more altar boys kept coming. We marched in, two by two, holding candles. Once I held the candle so close to my face that I singed my hair. Lined up at the foot of the altar, we would wait for Father to bring up the rear and take his place in the center. Everybody watched him because he was going to give the signal for us to genuflect together. When he clapped all 200 of us genuflected in unison. Then the majority of us filed into the two front-row pews, leaving the real serving to the high-school-age altar boys. Those were the boys who were going to be priests, I assumed, although I don't know if any of them did.

Fr. Snyder, who eventually took over for Fr. Huff,

held a special affinity for the altar boys. One day, he took us to a Minnesota Twins game at Met Stadium. We sat out in the cheap seats that constituted the left field bleachers; many of the boys couldn't sit still and took off to explore the park but Fr. Snyder didn't worry. He sat in the middle of a long row of seats, legs crossed with a program on his knee. Dressed in black, the small square of white on his collar identified him as a man of the cloth but tonight he was just one more sports fan. He recorded every play in his program. He even taught me the code for keeping tabs on the game. "6-4-3" meant the batter had hit into a double play. He wrote "1-3" when the batter grounded out to the pitcher. The game went into extra innings. We stayed until the end, although I know Father felt bad about getting us home so late since it was a school night.

By the time I got home from Des Moines, I was charged up about the Christianity Jim described. It seemed simpler than the Christianity I had learned as a kid. Over the next few weeks, I started reading the Bible and I threw out several hundred dollars worth of rock and roll albums. I stopped watching television and I promised myself I'd never go to another R-rated movie. I wanted to be on fire with my faith the way Jim Johnson was.

I spent a lot of time reading the Bible, like Jim said I should, but didn't understand most of it. I sought clarification from books I dug out of closets at my parents' home. Contradictions emerged. Jim pointed out to me that purgatory isn't mentioned anywhere in the Bible. Jesus did not set up a church with a pope, he told me. Nor did He tell people to confess their sins to a priest. But the books I found described purgatory, a hierarchal church, and seven sacraments including confession. The contradictions made me anxious. The enthusiasm I felt after that weekend with Jim began to wane.

Although I did a lot of reading to feed my spiritual hunger, most of my nourishment came from prayer. I didn't run into any conflicts when I prayed. Prayer brought me a certain amount of serenity, even if it didn't provide me with concrete answers about what to believe and how to live my life. Was the Holy Spirit moving my heart the way Jim said it would if I prayed? I didn't know. But I prayed.

As I thought about it, I had to acknowledge that almost everything I'd prayed for had come true. I'm still waiting on the big petitions, like world peace, a cure for cancer, and an end to selfishness, but on smaller things God has answered me, loud and clear. When Mom and Dad used to pray with us kids before bed, we'd end with petitions that usually went something like: "God, please bless Mom, Dad, Terri, Peggy, Tom, Bob and Jeanne, all our friends and relatives, and all those in need." After years and years of that kind of prayer, I think God really has blessed Mom, Dad, Terri, Peggy, Tom, Bob, and Jeanne, all our friends and relatives, and all those in need. Not that anyone in this group has avoided hardship but we have all lived richly blessed lives. With respect to "all those in need," I have always assumed that God is leaving the majority of the answer to me. If I help those in need, they will be blessed. If I ignore them, they will be ignored.

I have been praying for about as long as I can remember. Even during my least faith-filled years – college and a few years after – I prayed, albeit in a selfish way. "God, let me get this job ... make the pain go away ... help me make this putt." Prayer for so many years was a one-sided thing. I would do all the talking and I expected God to listen.

* * *

With Jim's encouragement, I thought a lot more about prayer and that thinking pushed me back to my roots — Catholicism. As in other areas of my life, I found myself returning to what I knew.

The church where I attended Mass offered "Eucharistic adoration," a purely Catholic concept where people come to the sanctuary to pray before the Eucharist. Bread, which has been consecrated into the Body of Christ, is put on display on an altar. At first the thought of praying before a communion host seemed strange but I realized that if I truly believed the bread to be the Body of Christ, then it made sense. What could be more appropriate than the created praising the Creator?

Soothed by the quiet of the empty church, I found that I love Eucharistic adoration. A spotlight shines on the monstrance, the gold and glass container that houses the Eucharist. Candles illuminate the room and the smell of wax comforts me. Sometimes, a faint scent of incense hangs in the air from a Mass earlier in the day. The stained-glass windows along the west wall of the church depict scenes from the life of Christ. The environment is beautiful and my goal is to settle my mind into a peace consistent with my surroundings. Usually I have a whole day of pressures, issues, and questions swirling in my head. Sometimes I have things to contemplate that have been percolating for days. My goal is to sit there, quietly. I have come to listen, not to talk — a new kind of prayer for me.

I listen but I don't know if I have ever heard anything. I don't expect a voice or a vision but I would like something. Oftentimes I come up with ideas that I would not have conceived in another setting. For example, one day I realized that the people washed away in the flood of Noah's day were probably a lot like 21st-century Americans. Another time, it occurred to me that when Jesus talks about a laborer gaining a full day's wage after working only a few hours in the vineyard, *He is talking about me!* Were these messages from God? Was the Almighty talking to me? Maybe.

Sometimes I catch myself sitting a little too casually, arms stretched along the back of the pew, my back slouched and legs crossed. I wouldn't sit this way in front of my boss. I'd sit more attentively in the presence of almost anyone; surely I can do better before my Maker. I spend a little time on my knees, the sparsely-padded kneeler making it possible for me to last no more than 20 minutes in the generally uncomfortable position. But something tells me I am supposed to be a little uncomfortable. This is when I find myself praying. I pray that journalists will find the courage to report the truth, that elected officials all over the world will work to move society into harmony with the truth, that teachers will show children what is beautiful in the world, and that orphaned children will find secure homes. I pray for my parents, my brother, and my sisters. I pray for friends and people everywhere who need help. I pray for wisdom and understanding. And I pray that God will give me faith.

When I was a little boy I used to pray that I could fly, a prayer that I had discontinued decades prior to signing up for flying lessons in the early 1990s. I took nearly two years of flight instruction at Flying Cloud, a little airport with two east/west runways and one north/south runway. I especially liked my early morning lessons in the summer, the ones that started at seven. The sun still would be low in the eastern sky, the smell of aviation fuel tingeing the calm air. Sometimes dew would sparkle in the grass that separated the taxi lanes from the runways.

I learned to fly a Piper Cherokee — a four-seat, low-wing airplane with a four-cylinder, 160-horse-power engine driving a single two-blade prop. The Warrior, the name of the Piper Cherokee I flew, is a much less complex vehicle than even the most economical new cars people buy today. Nonetheless, the airplane is a marvelous example of human achievement. Even though I understand the physics of heavier-than-air flight (when lift and acceleration exceed drag and weight, you get flight), I am still amazed that a 1,500-pound steel-and-plastic contraption can fly.

Part of the thrill of flying is sitting in the cockpit's left seat. A panel of dials and indicators provides a steady stream of information that the captain processes as he engages the aircraft's engine. When I flew by myself for the first time, I could hardly digest everything that was going on around me. I had had only 17 hours of flight training, which seemed like nothing to me. My instructor said it was a lot of time and that many people soloed with only a dozen hours of training.

I had arrived at Flying Cloud airport ready for another lesson when my instructor said, "Today's a good day to solo."

"It is?" I said. "It is."

We devised a flight plan that consisted of three takeoffs and landings. Seated next to me in the cockpit, the instructor said that all I had to do was fly in the pattern, an imaginary rectangular flight path over the airport. The sky was clear, there wasn't any wind, and there weren't many other airplanes using the field at the time. Once we agreed on what I would do he got up out of his seat and exited through the Warrior's only door. "Good luck," he told me. He was going to watch me from the control tower. "Good luck," I repeated to myself.

The first thing I did was make the sign of the cross and recite a Hail Mary. I spent a long time on the ramp going through my checklist, reviewing my flight pattern, and listening to the weather information. Finally I taxied to the edge of the ramp. I keyed my microphone: "Flying Cloud Tower, this is Warrior 4-5-6-8 Charlie at Thunderbird, staying in the pattern, with the information." I was cleared to taxi to runway 9, which meant that I would be taking off into the east. I taxied to the run-up area where airplanes test their engines. I hoped everything would go smoothly as I really didn't know what to do in the event something out of the ordinary should occur.

My engine checked out okay and I was cleared for takeoff. My heart was pounding when I threw the throttle forward. I released the brakes and began rolling down the runway. As my speed approached 55 knots, the nose lifted off the ground. Soon the main wheels followed and I was airborne. I was flying! There was a lot to think about as I tried to reach pattern altitude, which was 1,000 feet above the ground. I tried to keep an eye on my airspeed, aiming for 70 knots per hour, which gave me my best rate of climb at full throttle. I also watched the altimeter, which reported my elevation above sea level. At 300 feet above the ground I could return my flaps to normal. Everything went perfectly and I soon turned onto the "crosswind" leg of my pattern. I was beginning to enjoy this. Awe replaced nervousness. I looked at the buildings and cars on the ground. I began to think flying wasn't so hard. I turned again, this time onto the leg called "downwind," parallel to the runway.

Then the tower called. "Warrior 6-8 Charlie, we've got a runway change. You're cleared to land on runway 3-6."

"What!!!!" I said to myself. A runway change? This has never happened to me before.

The tower gets to designate which runway airplanes use when they land and take off, and it is almost always determined by the direction of the wind. Today, however, was calm so any runway would be safe. For some reason, the controllers decided to change runways and they decided to do it while I was flying – by myself for the first time in my life! I had never changed runways mid-pattern before. In fact, I had only landed on runway 36 a few times during my training. The vast majority of my takeoff and landing training was on the east/west runways. The north-south strip just wasn't used as much, given the typical wind patterns in the area. Landing on runway 36 meant flying final over the Minnesota River, where airplanes were known to catch strong updrafts created by a bluff just a few feet before the runway. I had been told that even on a calm day there could be updrafts. I could feel the perspiration forming on my forehead and under my arms.

I confirmed the runway change with the tower, turned to pick up the downwind leg of my new pattern, and asked the tower to "call my base." That means I left it up to them to tell me the best time to turn toward the runway. The controller gave me the signal and I flew the base leg of the pattern until I was perpendicular to the runway. I turned final on my own and prepared to land. The number 36 got larger and larger in my windshield as I approached the runway. I cleared the bluff and felt no updrafts. The aircraft eased onto the cement and I felt like a hero. I had flown by myself!

I had long forgotten my childhood prayer but, apparently, God had not.

※ ※ ※

Confession is a pillar of my faith. I love confession, a sacrament so attuned to human nature – a nature that cries out for an opportunity to tell people what we have done. Jim explained that Evangelicals may at times discuss transgressions with fellow believers but there is no obligation to make such disclosures to a clergyman. Whatever the variation, I derive a lot of good from confession, which I interpret as God's grace. Not that I especially like recounting my failings but it's like taking your medicine – you gotta do it to stay healthy. Anonymity in the confessional, like sugar in the medicine, makes it a little easier to take.

A Catholic begins the sacrament of confession by stepping in front of the mirror. Sometimes I can't bear to look. I know what I have done and I don't want to think about it. I want to wipe it out — put it in my past, so that I never have to deal with it again. I know I could be a better person and I want to be that person.

In the work world, the concept of self-evaluation is so well developed. Every business reviews its performance and makes changes to perform better in the future. This also happens at an individual level where employees are reviewed, with past performance analyzed and future goals established. Often, the employee is asked to review his own performance prior to the formal review with a superior. These are enormously useful practices for improving companies. Confession is a process for applying this self-evaluation and goal setting to one's personal life.

I know all this intellectually but sometimes I still avoid going. I am not afraid to face God in the confessional; I am afraid to face myself. God will forgive me — I know that — but will I forgive myself? Of course, I would be a fool not to; it is only pride and vanity that keeps me from being who I want to become. I confess those two sins first.

The German, Gothic-style church I attend is dark inside. The low light, the smell of burning candles, and the utter silence offers a perfect environment for penance. Usually, a line of people waits along the brick wall where the confessionals are located. Two confessionals, each no larger than a phone booth, are separated by a little room for the priest, who can talk to penitents through a cheesecloth-covered hole in the wall.

I wait in line until one of the confessionals frees up. While waiting, a prayer I learned in grade school loops in my head. "Oh my God, I am heartily sorry for having offended Thee ..." Sometimes I look at my watch while I wait. Conflicting feelings wage war in my gut. It is the same feeling I get in the waiting room at the doctor's office. I hate going to the doctor but I love being healthy. The wait is always longer than expected, and it only gives me time to dream up more things the doctor might find wrong with me. Sometimes when I am waiting for confession I secretly hope time will run out and the priest will emerge announcing "no more confessions today." That way, if I die in a car crash on my way home from church, I would still get the benefit of the sacrament, my intention having been there, but I would have avoided the excruciating process of sharing my sins.

But that never happens. In fact, the line moves quickly. Father is probably granting swift and easy absolution to all the old men and women who were bringing to him their minor transgressions. What sins could they possibly have? Maybe they over-ate once, or enjoyed the image of a scantily clad woman on television, or forgot to say a morning prayer. Why is it that most of the people who frequent confession are the people who hardly seem to need it? I suppose most people don't really believe that anything is a sin, so they don't go to confession. How come some people feel guilt and others don't?

Kneeling on the wooden plank at the floor triggers a light outside the confessional that tells those waiting that the room is occupied. At some churches the light is red; I always wondered if that represents the color of hell where you will burn if you don't confess all your sins. Inside, it is dark and stuffy. The walls are covered with a sound-absorbing material that is abrasive to the touch. But I am not looking around; I am looking ahead waiting for the window to open, where I would see a light from the priest's booth. Seconds pass and I hear the priest push back the screen that must run along a track on his side of the window. I launch into the verbiage I learned in second grade.

"Bless me Father for I have sinned. My last confession was two months ago. My sins are pride, vanity, profanity, illicit desire, lack of compassion, ingratitude …"

These are ugly admissions. It would be so easy to deny any responsibility for these actions, claiming to be the victim of circumstance. Yes, I swore, but I was angry. And what man doesn't sometimes fantasize about the beautiful women he sees? Catholicism is so strict. Like everyone else at Mass, I strike my breast, praying: "I have sinned through my own fault, in my thoughts and in my words, in what I have done and in what I have failed to do." Can anyone be innocent under such intense self-examination? Certainly I'm not. Furthermore, scripture says that any man who looks upon another woman with lust has already committed adultery in his heart. What a standard! Confession is the only way out. Of course I try to do what is right, but I fail. Forgiveness is my only hope.

I keep my voice low in the confessional, which is difficult for me. Once, the priest had a hearing disability and he asked me to repeat myself. I hated that. It was hard enough to verbalize my sins the first time, let alone a second time a little bit louder.

Sometimes I wonder if the priest recognizes my voice. Does he know who I am? What must a priest think of a person who time after time brings the same sins before God? Can a person really be repentant if he keeps doing the same things wrong, over and over again? Confession doesn't just mean saying you're sorry, it means resolving to avoid those sins in the future. Clearly I fail.

The point is moot though, because the priest always grants absolution. Sometimes, he offers a few words of encouragement for fighting the temptation to sin in the future. The ritual concludes with a prayer of absolution and an exchange of "Amen" and "thank you." Finding a pew, I kneel, pray and I thank God for His mercy. Sometimes the priest asks me to do something, in addition to praying, to complete my confession … something like a good deed for an elderly person or an act of kindness for a family member. I have to think about what I am going to do, and how to get it done as quickly as possible.

* * *

In 1987, two years after my July weekend in Des Moines with Jim Johnson, my sister Jeanne and I visited Europe where we toured the Cathedral of Notre Dame in Paris. The tour guide pointed out a stone carving located above the main doors at the front of the church. Depicted is a woman surrounded by books. In front of her is a ladder, leading above her head, into the sky. Just above the ladder is a cloud. The guide explained the symbolism of the image. He said the woman represents knowledge. As we obtain more knowledge, we climb the ladder, moving closer to heaven, which is represented by the cloud. However, even if we learn all there is to know, reaching the top of the ladder, there is still a leap required to reach heaven — the leap of faith. The point of the carving is to show that with knowledge the leap is smaller and easier to make. This is certainly true for me; as I learn more about life and Catholicism, I find it easier to make a leap of faith.

5

Vows

At the age of 26, a girlfriend had just dumped me and I found myself commiserating with my mother – a woman who seemed to be able to solve all my problems when I was a boy. Seated at her kitchen table, Mom asked me about the status of several women we knew in common – most of whom I hadn't seen since eighth grade.

"What about Debbie? She's cute," Mom asked. "Or how about Kelly? She's a real doll. Or there's Cindy. I've always thought she was good looking."

"Mom, it doesn't matter what they look like," I had to clarify. "That's not what I'm after."

"Then what are you looking for?" she asked.

"All I want is someone who will listen to me and be interested in the things I have to say."

Mom, who could be brutally honest, looked me straight in the eye. "Tom, that's asking an awful lot."

* * *

Some months later, I walked into the director's office at the University of Minnesota's school of journalism where Susan Kjos was sitting behind the counter. We were meeting for lunch that July 13, 1987, a blind date set up by one of Susan's co-workers who worked with me when I was at the U.

I shook Susan's hand upon our introduction, seeking elusive eye contact. Was she ignoring me, or was she a little nervous? I was wearing a tie, which set me apart from the J-school students in the office. Maybe the tie was intimidating but I wanted Susan to know that I was not a student. I was past college. I was in the real world, doing real-world things like earning a living and looking for a lifelong mate.

Susan struck me as cute – petite, brown hair, blue-green eyes, and small feet. I liked her shape and I liked the feel of her warm hand in mine as we said hello. I was already pretty sure I wanted to see her again.

"Blind dates can be awkward," I offered.

"They can be," Susan said.

We walked outside and made our way to Annie's Parlor. There was a nervous silence as we left Murphy Hall but by the time we got to the restaurant, we had a conversation going – or maybe it was an interview. I peppered her with questions. I wanted to know everything about her, and she gave me answers that I liked. Born in Wauwatosa, Wisconsin, the second of four children, Susan grew up in a neighborhood full of kids. She learned to ride a bike at 5 years of age, was the neighborhood champion at marbles, could bounce on a pogo stick for 30 minutes, and earned a sash-full of badges in her Girl Scout troop.

Susan's father took a new job in Minneapolis in 1980 and moved the family to Minnesota. For Susan, the move divided her high school experience; old friendships were disrupted and new ones formed only slowly as she found it nearly impossible to overcome the "new kid" label that a cliquish student population pegged on her at Armstrong High School. College at the University of Minnesota offered her a fresh start. Susan lived on campus, enjoying the social benefits of the Pi Beta Phi sorority house, where her mother and grandmother had been members before her. She had graduated only a year earlier and was still trying to figure out what to do with the degree she had earned in international relations and French. She told me she was in the process of applying for a job with a foreign exchange program where she would have to find host families in the Twin Cities for high school students traveling here from France.

"What do you do for fun?" I asked.

"I like to golf," she said. "I have been golfing for years. How about you?"

"My dad golfs a lot, and I play a little," I said.

"I am going to give you my telephone number," she said, writing on a scrap of paper. "Call me some time and we can play a round of golf together."

I stuffed the scrap of paper into my shirt pocket and said I would call, thinking how nice it would be to spend five hours outdoors on a summer afternoon with her.

* * *

But it was a month before I called, taking a three-week trip to Europe with Jeanne in the interim – the trip where I visited the Notre Dame Cathedral. I thought about Susan the whole time, wondering if she might be the one. Susan, like me, wanted to recreate the happy experience of her childhood. I knew I was ready for marriage. I had a good job and a place to live. I knew what I wanted and I fantasized that Susan was it. Upon returning, I immediately invited Susan over to my apartment.

"Nice stereo," she commented as she made herself comfortable in my home, and in my life.

I offered her a cup of tea and she loved it. The service, I mean, more than the tea itself. Other benign dates followed. On the fourth date we kissed – a passionate exchange on my couch that made up for a month of polite distance. I thought she tasted like heaven. I held her in my arms and ran my hands through that curly hair I had been thinking about for weeks. I was falling in love, and I was hoping Susan was too.

A parental introduction was the logical next step.

I wanted them to hit it off and I wasn't going to leave success to chance so I instructed Susan to score points with my dad by asking him about his golf game. She did and it turned out to be a great ice-breaker. The next summer, Dad invited Susan and me to play golf with him. On the first tee, I dribbled the ball into the rough, as I often do. Susan got up there and pelted the ball 200 yards down the center of the fairway. Dad elbowed me, saying "great back swing!" Susan played a good round of golf and they have been friends ever since.

I had dated several women during my 20s only to discover after a few outings that I had little in common with them. It would become obvious that we didn't think alike. As I got older, this kind of dating seemed to be a big waste of time so when I started going out with Susan I took an all-or-nothing gamble. Susan and I, taking advantage of a beautiful sunset, were walking around Lake Calhoun. We found a bench, sat down and I began to talk. For the next 45 minutes I delivered a monologue in which I communicated all the things I believed. I told her about my faith in God, my renewed interest in Catholicism, my desire to serve God with my life, and more. When I was done we just looked at each other and then she wrapped her arms around me; we hugged for a long time. Susan, raised Catholic, had not thought very much about her faith. I think she saw me as someone who could lead her on a lifelong faith journey. We didn't talk a lot after my monologue that night but Susan grew closer to me. She did not move away, nor leave as I had feared. I knew right then Susan was the woman for me. She was like the woman I told my mom I wanted. Susan listened to what I had to say and was interested.

But equally important, I found myself listening to Susan. She was clever, hardworking, and fun. She described traditional political and cultural philosophies that matched mine, and she said she had no idea where they came from because her parents were so overtly liberal. "Susan — a rebel," I thought. That was kind of cool for me because I was the exact opposite. I didn't rebel against my parents, but tried to become like them. Whereas I went to the local college so I could continue living at home, Susan moved out immediately upon entering college. She said she didn't even call home that first year away until about Thanksgiving. Yet, she clearly loved her parents. I saw the care she took selecting gifts for birthdays and holidays. I saw how polite she was around them, even when her mom would go on about some political issue Susan had no interest in. And I saw how respectful she was toward her grandparents, demonstrating incredible patience with their deteriorating physical capabilities.

Plus, Susan was honest, something I realized on the golf course.

"You don't have to count that shot," I told Susan after she put a drive out of bounds. "Take a mulligan."

"Mulligans are for cheaters," she said. "I'll take my two-stroke penalty."

"You don't have to do that to impress me," I said. "This is just a friendly game. Plus, if you count every penalty stroke, you'll make me feel guilty if I don't do the same."

"That's the idea," she said. "You can't lie just because something seems unimportant. If you lie on the golf course, next thing you know you're lying on your tax return."

She recorded her penalty strokes and still beat me that round by nine strokes.

* * *

Susan and I had been dating for about a year when I had a dream in which she and I were laughing together on a balcony. We were smiling and our eyes were sparkling. I held a bottle of *Veuve Clicquot* between us, and we each held a champagne glass. As Susan and I nuzzled, I worked the cork off the bottle. It exploded with a loud pop. The cork flew 40 feet into the air, landing a half a mile away. Streams of white bubbly followed, spilling over us. We laughed some more and drank the sweet, intoxicating juice. I woke up in a sweat with no doubt in my mind. I needed to marry Susan.

The next morning, I went into work and the publisher of the magazine made me an offer. The Independent Community Bankers of America was set to convene its annual convention in Hawaii. "I'd like you to cover the meeting, Tom," he told me. "Get one of those charter deals. It will be a lot less expensive than using the regular commercial service. And take your girlfriend if you want. It's almost as cheap for two people to go to Hawaii as one."

Wow, what an offer! I completely forgot everything I told Susan during my monologue and invited her to Hawaii with me. Susan was elated. She told all her friends I was taking her to Hawaii.

I didn't want to hide the trip from my family so at a gathering at Mom and Dad's house, I told them I was going to Hawaii with Susan. I remember Terri reacting politely. Dad said nothing. Mom said maybe we could hang a sheet up in the hotel room to divide it for privacy.

The next day, Dad telephoned me at my apartment after work.

"I suppose you know you dropped a real bombshell on us yesterday," he said.

I wasn't sure what he was talking about. Then he said I shouldn't go to Hawaii with Susan.

Long, silent pause.

I did not argue with him, nor try to defend myself. "If you don't want me to go with her, I won't," I responded.

Dad was a little surprised by how easily I went along with him. I was, too, at the moment but as I thought about it later, I guess I realized I couldn't disappoint my father. I knew he was right and I had to listen to him. I could hear relief in his voice as he further told me that such a trip would set a bad example for the other family members. Dad even offered to pay for Susan's nonrefundable airplane ticket but I declined.

Now I had to tell Susan that I was backing out on my offer to take her to Hawaii. I thought she might leave me over this but I figured it was kind of like my monologue – if she dumped me, it wasn't meant to be.

Fact is, she did not dump me, although I know she was disappointed. The hardest thing for Susan was telling her friends. Many of them told her she should get a new boyfriend. Only a horrible man would promise a woman something like that and then renege, they said. I am grateful she didn't listen to them.

* * *

Susan, who struck me from the start with her sincerity and goodness, reminded me so much of my mother. Rose Anne Danko, born in Randall, Minnesota in 1930, doesn't like to talk about what must have been a difficult childhood. The younger of two kids, she lived in a small house heated with a wood-burning stove and lighted with kerosene lamps; there was no indoor plumbing. Mom says they only had one wind-up clock in the house and it

often was inaccurate. She was so nervous about missing the school bus that she would arrive at the bus stop 90 minutes early. Diligent and hard working, Mom told me she was never so devastated as when her teacher asked everyone in the class to write a report on their favorite radio program. Mom was too embarrassed to admit that her family didn't have a radio, so she made something up and was torn apart inside for years about lying to her teacher. I thought of Susan, who studied so hard in college that her mother had to remind her to go out and have a good time every now and then.

Mom's main form of entertainment on the farm was paging through the Sears catalog and dreaming about a better life. But for her father, George Danko, this was a better life. He left starvation and oppression in Slovakia to make his way to Minneapolis where he found work in the flour mills. He lost a finger working one of the machines and decided to return to what he knew best, farming. Land ownership, after all, was the real symbol of success. With his wife, Anna, George found a farm in central Minnesota where locals sold these outsiders a wild team of plow horses. While the neighbors sat back and laughed, George tried to get those stubborn beasts to tow a plow. It took time, but he was more stubborn than the horses and he got his crop in. Every year, he'd be the first one to harvest. Mom said George was a proud man, who worked hard and made his own way. They say girls grow into women and marry their fathers; Rose Anne left Randall and married Frank Bengtson in 1958.

Perhaps rebelling against the size of their childhood families, Frank and Rose had five children in six years. I was number three, behind Terri, the smart one, and Peggy, who could have passed for my twin. Had I been born at home like my mother was, Bob and Jeanne would never have come along. After two  easy births, mine was complicated and Mom would have died had the scene played out a decade or two earlier. Modern medicine saved her, as it did me eight years later when I nearly died of an infection. Thank goodness for the wisdom of doctors!

In fall 1988, I asked Susan to marry me. Having obtained a diamond ring and the blessing of her parents, I showed up at Susan's apartment unannounced. With Susan sitting on the couch, I got down on one knee and proposed. I not only asked her to marry me but told her how much I loved her, how I would work to make a nice home, how I would treat her well and on and on and on. My chattiness revealed a high degree of nervousness. Susan later told me she would gladly have accepted my proposal right away but I didn't give her a chance to respond for at least 15 minutes.

Emerging Son

* * *

During our engagement, Susan and I took a class to learn about natural family planning, a method of reading physical clues to determine whether a woman is fertile. This is important information for couples that want to live according to the Catholic faith, which prohibits the use of birth control. The physical signs of fertility were easy enough to learn: the texture of cervical mucus changes prior to ovulation and body temperature rises after ovulation. Women are fertile only two days following ovulation and sperm lives for about five days. Studies show couples using this information can avoid pregnancy as reliably as they can by using the pill.

The class, taught by devoted Catholic volunteers, offered more than just physiology. At least two hours of instruction were devoted to theology. They must have been reading my mind, where the "why" was more important than the "how." They explained that sexual intercourse includes two inseparable components, which the Catholic Church labels "procreative" and "unitive." The concept comes out of the first two chapters of scripture, where the first relationship between a man and a woman is described. Genesis 1 is a creation story that concludes with God commanding Adam and Eve to "be fruitful and multiply." This represents the procreative component. Genesis 2 is a creation story as well; it concludes with God creating Eve from the rib of

Adam. The two satisfy their loneliness by clinging together. This represents the unitive component. The
Church argues that both creation stories are equally
important, and neither can be ignored. The parallel is
that couples cannot focus on one component of the
marital embrace to the exclusion of the other.

This education brought so much of Catholicism
into focus for me. I began to see, for example, how sex
outside marriage could be a crime against God. The
Church understands how counter-cultural chastity is
and that is one reason it provides so many examples of
chaste living. The celibate priesthood, based on the example of Christ Himself, is meant to be an inspiration
to people called to chastity – which, in fact, is most
people: single folks, and even married people a few days
per month if they are unprepared for children. Catholics, furthermore, even believe Mary and Joseph lived a
celibate marriage. Susan and I wouldn't be following
their example, but we drew inspiration from it.

＊ ＊ ＊

Susan and I were married on August 26, 1989. So
many disparate thoughts darted in and out of my head
that Saturday before the 2 p.m. wedding. I recalled Mr.
Bjallin, the funny round man who fell in our driveway
when I was a kid. He had a wife every bit as much of a
character as he was. They owned a big car that Mrs.
Bjallin would drive to the grocery store. Even with the

seat moved all the way forward, Mrs. Bjallin's head barely reached higher than the top of the steering wheel. She was a careful driver who never approached the speed limit. Many times while I played basketball in the driveway with Bob and my sisters, we would see Mrs. Bjallin approaching in her car from the west. She drove toward us on 54th Street, taking a half a block to slow from her 20-miles-per-hour speed to a virtual stop in front of our driveway where she would begin her left turn. Her garage was about half way down the block along the alley that accommodated several telephone poles and everyone's garbage cans, including those belonging to another neighbor, Mrs. Kelly. Invariably, Mrs. Bjallin would attempt the turn and stop after crashing the right front corner of her car into Mrs. Kelly's garbage cans. Mrs. Bjallin would throw the vehicle into reverse, pull her bumper out of Mrs. Kelly's trashcans, and proceed forward through the remainder of the turn. In all the years we lived in that house, Mrs. Kelly always had dented garbage cans.

Sitting in the basement of St. Olaf's Church, I wondered what would happen if Susan and I ended up like the Bjallins. Was it possible that I would turn into the neighborhood character, married to an equally goofy woman? Was there still life left in the Bjallins's relationship, who surely had been married 50 or more years? What if years in the future, I retain my mental faculties and my wife goes nuts, unable to do even simple things like make a left turn at five miles per hour? Am I the kind of man who could stand by my wife no matter what happened? Could I be as good a man as Mr. Bjallin? I hoped so, since I was about to declare my lifelong love for Susan in front of everyone I knew.

I also thought about Mrs. Dalberg, who lived across 54th Street. She had a corner lot, surrounded with sidewalk. Plus she had a double garage with a huge driveway. All that pavement impressed me because Bob and I used to shovel snow for her. A storm would dump eight inches of snow on the neighborhood and Bob and I would spend four hours shoveling out Mrs. Dalberg, who lived alone. We didn't mind the shoveling so much; it was the after-shoveling visit that made us uncomfortable. We'd ring her doorbell to inform her that we had completed the job, and wait to be paid. She would invite us in to talk. It was a one-sided conversation in which she would tell us about her ailments, doctor visits, and other problems. It was always a depressing monologue. Once I asked her how long she had been feeling so down.

"For years," she answered. "Ever since my husband died."

How would I feel if I lost Susan? I wondered as I adjusted my cummerbund. I had never really faced the death of a close friend or relative before. How would I handle the death of my spouse? Would I be able to get on with my life or would it paralyze me? And what if Susan outlived me? How would she react? Watching from the afterlife, would I want her to happily carry on, perhaps even remarry? Or would it please me to see her mourn indefinitely over my death?

The Sunday edition of the *New York Times* includes a column called "Vows." I read it ahead of sports, opinion, and international news every week. The column introduces us to some random couple getting married, offering details about how they met, what kinds of things are important to them, what they work at, and what they hope for the future. A big picture of the happy couple usually accompanies the column. They always look so cheerful, so hopeful, but many times I wondered about the things that the author left out. For example, many of the weddings constituted a second marriage for one or both of the parties. What about that first spouse? What happened to her? Was she starting her life over somewhere with a happy partner? Could anyone really forget a first spouse and start their life over? Marriage is a very complicated thing. Marriage, divorce and remarriage is surely far more complicated.

I couldn't avoid asking myself, "what was I about to get myself into?" One of the readings we considered for our wedding Mass said: "Husbands, love your wives as Christ loves the Church." Our priest told me that Christ loved the Church so much that He died for it. I was, therefore, expected to be willing to die for my wife. Wow! Well, I suppose if an armed robber threatened my wife, I'd be willing to step in front of her and take a bullet if I had to. Sure, I'd do that for Susan.

And I kind of wondered what would happen to my hormones after I got married. Would they calm down any? A ceremony in front of all my friends and family, vows before God and my priest, a $10,000 reception ... would this guarantee my faithfulness? Would other women no longer appear attractive to me? I wished I could have talked to my dad about this. He always seemed like the perfect husband, completely devoted to Mom. Did he ever look at another woman and wonder? I'll never know. I can talk to Dad about power tools and sports and business, but not sex and sin.

Marriage is a big deal. I would now have to work harder than ever to remain committed to Susan. We wouldn't just be dating any more. It seemed to me that our relationship was about to grow into something bigger than just Susan and me having a good time. We'd be married, 'til death do us part.

I remembered Galatians 5, which says that living in God's love means we need to "die unto Christ" by turning our back on the desires of the flesh. So if I was going to make this marriage work, I'd have to turn my back on lust, the sin I had so often confessed. When it was just my own soul at stake, perhaps I was content with only a little resistance, knowing forgiveness and absolution was readily available. But now my wife would be involved; her trust in me was at stake. Loving Susan as Christ loved the Church probably had a lot more to do with dedicating myself to purity and fidelity than it did with stepping in front of a gunman's bullet.

Interrupting my thoughts, my father joined Bob and me in the waiting room 30 minutes before the wedding. Susan was upstairs with her personal attendant and three bridesmaids posing for pictures. Dad came over to me and shook my hand.

"I have a little advice," he told me.

"What is it, Dad?"

"Anything your wife wants, just do it," he told me.

I didn't respond. He slapped me on the back and walked out of the room.

✳ ✳ ✳

If the Vows column had featured Susan and me, the reporter would have noted that Susan wore a floor-

length, beaded white dress, with a veil and a very long train. The groom was attired in a traditional black tuxedo with tails. Three bridesmaids wore teal dresses and carried small bouquets. The groomsmen also wore black tuxes, although without the tails. It was a traditional Catholic wedding in the main sanctuary at St. Olaf Church in downtown Minneapolis. In addition to approximately 200 invited guests, a dozen or so street people attended the ceremony, watching from a back row pew. Male and female vocalists sang Michael Joncas' *On Eagles Wings* and other contemporary songs. The male singer doubled as a trumpet player, and an organist provided traditional music for the opening and closing. Fr. Paul Sirba, a high school tennis partner to the groom, presided at the Mass and witnessed the wedding. A reception that included a champagne toast, dinner, and dancing, followed in the evening at Rolling Green Country Club, a golf course about 20 miles west of downtown.

Susan and I left the next day for a two-week honeymoon in Canada. We flew to Montreal, drove to Quebec, and reveled in the fine food, dazzling sightseeing, and first-time experiences alone. We stayed at the Chateau Frontenac in Quebec City, a European castle-like hotel that made us feel like a king and queen. We must have been glowing because more than once strangers interrupted us on the street to ask if we were on our honeymoon.

We spent a few nights in bed & breakfast hotels, and Susan and I noticed that most of the other couples were unmarried. The conversation at the communal breakfast always gave them away. They appeared quite happy, none of them exhibiting any uneasiness about their nontraditional traveling arrangements. It struck me that any one of these couples could have been Susan and me in Hawaii. Maybe these other couples didn't have parents like mine. And I wondered: Was I better than the people across the table because I had parents who took a traditional moral stand? Would they have laughed at Susan and me if they knew we complied? But why should I care what anyone thinks? Morality is rarely a matter of popularity. When we returned home, I told Susan how glad I was that we were married, and I realized I loved my parents a little bit more.

* * *

Shortly after the wedding, Susan and I joined the Couple to Couple League, the organization that provided the teachers for the natural family planning class we took. We volunteered to help with the organization's promotional efforts. That means we were expected to come up with ways to promote natural family planning, a topic that most people don't understand nor want to talk about. The standard public relations activities included making presentations at parish events, writing articles for parish bulletins or religious newspapers, and staffing displays at faith-oriented seminars and retreats. Susan and I, however, were full of energy and had lots of new ideas. Surely we could come up with more dynamic ways to get the word out. We brought two ideas to the organization's leadership: billboards and direct mail.

I always liked billboards because "outdoor media," as the advertising professionals call it, is nonintrusive. The message is simply presented and a passerby can choose to look at it or look the other way. So we encouraged the Couple to Couple League to appropriate $10,000 for a modest billboard campaign. This was a monumental amount of money for an all-volunteer organization that typically saved aluminum cans for the recycling revenue, but we figured we could raise the money if we tried. We got the "okay" and over the course of a year, we placed about 10 billboards around the city. The message said: "Natural Family Planning – it works!" The ad was meant to respond to the commonly held falsehood that it is impossible to determine periods of fertility. The green and yellow ads carried a phone number and the CCL logo.

The billboard company we used had no idea what our message was about. One of the account execs even told me natural family planning was a crock, something she knew, she said, "because my husband is a doctor." She must have ignored the organization's stationery I used to correspond with her; along one side, it listed a whole bunch of doctors on the Couple to Couple League's advisory board. Another account exec helped us select locations for our messages. We scored big with billboards that went up near the State Fair and the Uptown Art Fair. These events drew thousands of people, which meant we got exceptional visibility for our message. One suggested location, however, didn't work out. The account exec told me he had a location available at 27th Street and Hennepin Avenue.

Something about that address stuck in my mind so I asked him to hold off until I had time to check it out. I drove by the corner, finding the billboard. It was located atop a building that housed a store called the "Condom Kingdom." We elected not to use that site.

To complement the billboard effort, Susan and I embarked on a direct mail campaign for the Couple to Couple League. I went to the Hennepin County records office and reviewed recently filed marriage certificates. Those that indicated a marriage officiated by a clergy-man were of interest to me. I recorded the names of the couples and their addresses. The Couple to Couple League's public relations committee then sent each of these couples a letter congratulating them on their marriage. The letter concluded with an invitation to take a class in natural family planning. I signed about 1,000 such letters that we mailed out over the course of the campaign.

Neither the billboard campaign nor our direct mail effort resulted in any increase in class sizes. In fact, we may have done more harm than good. Some people didn't understand our billboard messages and assumed by our name – Couple to Couple League – that we were promoting wife swapping. Other people called to complain about the letters. They said it was offensive to address something so personal in a letter. I never meant to be offensive but any time you encourage someone to think about what they believe and how they intend to reflect that in their life, you risk making them uncomfortable. Recalling that phone call to my apartment about Hawaii, I am sure Dad knew he'd be making me uncomfortable. But he shared his convictions nonetheless and I am glad he did.

6

Business School

I liked my job at *Commercial West* magazine but I kept thinking about my dad, who owned his own business. I wanted to own my own business and be a success like Dad was, and I thought *Commercial West* might give me that chance. It was a relatively small business and I understood it thoroughly; if I could buy it, I would gain independence that most people only dream of. And I wanted Dad to be proud of me. I had tried to imitate Dad in other ways and it just didn't work out. Dad could fix anything with his own two hands; I was a mechanical klutz who couldn't even explain how the furnace worked. Dad was a good golfer and instructed me in the game from my childhood but I never really caught on. But maybe I could run my own business.

I got my chance beginning on March 4, 1992, when I purchased the magazine and started NFR Communications. Paul Blackburn was the seller. He had purchased *Commercial West* in 1987 and a year later, its Des

Moines-based competitor, *Northwestern Banker*, merging the two into a new magazine he called *Northwestern Financial Review*. Blackburn had done a lot of good at the magazine – taking out a competitor with the merger, going to an every-other-week format from a weekly, and starting new editorial features. But Blackburn's heart was not in publishing. He was a hands-off manager who would go weeks at a time without checking into the office. I had a hunch he'd sell the magazine if a good offer came along and I wanted to be the guy to make that offer.

Blackburn's lead salesperson was Bob Cronin, who came to the company through *Northwestern Banker*. I had known Bob since 1985 when we were competitors covering the same industry meetings. When Blackburn purchased *Northwestern Banker*, these two rivals became colleagues.

Blackburn tried to grow his publishing business with other publications. He had gotten involved in producing an in-flight magazine for Mesaba Airlines, a venture that never took off (pardon the pun). Then he tried to buy a five-day-a-week business newspaper called *Finance and Commerce*. That deal fell through and it really got him down. I made a passing comment to Paul at the time that if he ever wanted to sell the magazine he should let me know.

"You want to buy the magazine?" Blackburn asked. "Make me an offer."

Wow! That was easy. Blackburn really wanted to

sell! Of course, I had no money nor any knowledge about how to put a deal together. I told Blackburn I would come up with something and make an offer soon.

Blackburn told me Cronin also wanted to buy the magazine, so the two of us quickly agreed to combine resources and work together. But before we could do anything, we needed a few answers. What was the magazine worth? How reliable was the information Blackburn was giving us? What percentage of stock would each of us own? How much should the down payment be? Where would we get the money?

Blackburn provided us with old tax returns and he said he wanted $70,000 down. As a rule of thumb, he said, magazines typically attract a price near their annual revenue or five times their net income, a guideline we learned to be meaningless considering the magazine wasn't making money.

The negotiations progressed rapidly. We agreed on a price, which we considered to be a bargain in light of the potential we saw in *Northwestern Financial Review*. Bob and I each had to come up with $35,000 to make the down payment; I used $10,000 of savings and borrowed $25,000 from my dad. We presented our offer around Thanksgiving time and by early March we had closed on the sale.

Cronin and I ended up being 50-50 shareholders. I originally proposed a 51 percent / 49 percent split but Bob refused, saying he had seen his old boss at the *Northwestern Banker* suffer as a minority owner. Nonetheless, for a marriage of convenience, the Cronin/ Bengtson partnership initially proved remarkably productive. We quickly moved the company's Minneapolis office to a smaller space to trim the substantial lease payment we had inherited. We found other ways to save costs and Bob ramped up the ad sales. I made interest-only payments to my father for the first several months after the purchase and in December I handed him a check for $25,000 to pay off my debt to him. I think Dad was really proud of me.

My first day of magazine ownership, I had to figure out how to be a boss. I had been so focused on closing the deal that I failed to spend much time thinking about how I would manage the staff. A salesperson and three other employees came with the deal, and I sensed their apprehension from the beginning; perhaps they sensed mine, as my management experience was limited. We had worked together as peers and it wasn't easy for everyone to accept, overnight, the fact that I was now their boss.

Bob and I fired the salesperson right away and this didn't do anything to add to anyone's comfort about our management style – although it should have, as it was a prudent business decision. Bob had planned all along to handle the advertising sales by himself. The Twin Cities salesman barely sold enough to cover his own salary and we had informed Blackburn long before the deal closed that we did not intend to maintain two salespeople.

While the firing may have left the others worrying about their own job security, I was hoping the action would send a positive signal that Bob and I were hands-on managers who deeply cared about the success of the company. As a hands-off manager, Blackburn left the impression he didn't care about the company's performance. He took little interest in banking and even less interest in publishing details like subscription drives, desktop publishing software, production schedules, and editorial formats. I cared a lot about the banking industry and wanted to learn everything I could about publishing.

But my enthusiasm wasn't infectious. No one seemed impressed by my interest in the company, attention to detail, knowledge of the market, nor editorial ability. Staff meetings were awkward. We'd sit around the table and people would stare at me. When they did respond, they always left me wanting. Most of the time they didn't say much during the meetings and the nonverbal communication was deafening.

I knew why some people were uneasy. They didn't like the fact that I was asking employees to start their day by briefing me on what they planned to do for the next eight hours. I started this ritual because I wanted to know what everyone did and I figured it would be a great way for me to learn all the ins and outs of the business. I explained my purpose but it wasn't enough to help some of the employees get over their idea that I was being nosey. And some employees were upset that we moved the office to a smaller space. From my perspective, the move was an essential cost-saver – an unsatisfying reason for staff that just assumed Bob and I were getting rich at the expense of their comfortable working environment.

In the end, I failed to win over any of the original employees. By year-end 1992, all the employees who came with the purchase were gone. Two left on their own and we fired one more in addition to the salesman. Under previous ownership, the magazine had experienced a high rate of turnover and I really hoped to change that. I was off to a poor start. Maybe, I thought, I'd do better hiring my own people.

During the next several years, staffing turned out to be the toughest part of managing the business. Many people came and went, most willing only to do the bare minimum amount of work to keep from getting fired — and a few were unwilling to do even that much. I found the hiring process to be extremely frustrating. I'd run a classified ad in the Help Wanted section of the Sunday newspaper, collect resumes, interview a few candidates, pick one and hope for the best. Most employees would stay about two years before moving on to something else, frustrating me to no end since two years is about as much time as a person needs to learn how to do their job well.

As the boss over the years, I tried being firm; I

tried being a consensus builder; I tried all kinds of things to keep the employees happy. The latest best-selling management books offer guys like me all kinds of advice on how to run a business. Young and eager to succeed, I read a lot of those books and tried whatever was the management philosophy of the week. Many of the gurus talked about "empowering" employees, "flattening" the organizational chart, viewing employees as partners instead of subordinates. "Okay," I thought. At one point we had several staff meetings to talk about how to make NFR Communications better, about how the company could offer more fulfilling work experiences. All the employees agreed they needed a retirement savings plan. The big disadvantage to working at NFR Communications, they said, was there was no 401(k) plan. That's why no one stayed more than a year or two. "Hmmm," I thought.

Within a few months, I found a company that could set up a 401(k) plan for NFR Communications. I announced the move with fanfare. I remember the investment representative coming to our office, telling the staff about our "global investment options." He told us we could divide our investment into "baskets" minimizing our risk, and "diversify our assets." The staff listened and collected numerous color-coded prospectuses – blue for bond funds, red for equities, and gray for index funds. Including the pricey annual testing, that 401(k) plan cost the company a lot of money.

The effort proved to be worthless. Two of the

employees who were so adamant about wanting the plan left six months after we set it up. The others declined to participate – and we were offering an employer match. Go figure! Turned out I was one of only two people in the plan. I felt totally hoodwinked by the whole business. I can see now that it makes no sense to give people the opportunity to vote themselves more money and benefits because, of course, that's exactly what they'll do — without any consideration for its impact on the rest of the company.

Keeping up with developments in technology was another big challenge. Computers have so changed the publishing business in the last decade. It used to take three people to do the design and layout work that one skilled person with good computer equipment can do now. I remember working at the *Enterprise* on a boxy computer with a tiny green-tinted display screen. Copy was recorded onto big floppy disks that were given to production personnel. They fed the disks into other machines that spit out long strips of film that contained the stories in two- and three-inch columns. The production people would apply wax to the back of the strips, cut them to size and then paste them together on a page like a jigsaw puzzle. Headlines were produced by a keyboard contraption that looked like Mr. Peabody's time machine. A big dial could be turned to indicate headlines of varying size. And a switch gave operators the option of selecting italicized type. The machine didn't have a visual display, so you would type the headline in, wait a few minutes for the machine to process, and watch it emit a strip containing the line of type. Inevitably, there would be a spelling mistake and the whole effort would have to be repeated. When the headline finally came out right, it would be waxed, trimmed, and fit into the puzzle, which became the newspaper that day. What a difference today, when an entire newspaper or magazine can be formatted on a colorful computer screen and digitized for transmission over the Internet.

The Internet has changed the publishing business more than anything and I have mixed feelings about that. Reporting is so much easier now that we have libraries of information at our fingertips. But the Internet also lulls reporters into lazy habits. A reporter can get a lot of stories surfing the Internet but the best stories are uncovered through face-to-face contact and personal interaction. If you rely solely on the Internet, you'll get the same stories that everyone else gets; if you visit with bankers, attend the meetings, and talk to bank customers and regulators in person, you will get stories that others miss. Of course, this method is a lot more work than surfing the web but, then, good reporting isn't supposed to be easy.

✳ ✳ ✳

Bob Cronin would sometimes refer to our partnership in flattering terms like Lewis and Clark or the

Wright Brothers, but that overstated the case. We had some wonderful experiences working and traveling together, and we had some success turning *Northwestern Financial Review*'s profit picture around, but I had serious concerns about the company's long-term viability. Bob wasn't the kind of guy who adapted to change easily nor was he comfortable with risk, but I believed change and risk were inevitable. New products and services were essential to NFR Communications' long-term survival as I was convinced *Northwestern Financial Review* magazine would not grow sufficiently on its own to sustain our company. While I believed in the need to invest in the future, Bob didn't always see it that way; he believed we had already made a substantial investment in the company and now he wanted to cash in.

Having been uncomfortable with the 50-50 ownership arrangement from the beginning, I approached Bob around Christmas 1995 to encourage him to sell his half to me. I suggested he form his own company, perhaps an advertising rep firm. I'd sign on as his first customer and he could go on selling for *Northwestern Financial Review*. By forming his own specialized company, I figured Bob would get the chance to focus on what he did best, which was sell. With me as his first client, he'd have a good base for launching his business.

I was surprised at how quickly he latched onto the idea. Shortly after the first of the year in 1996 he gave me a proposal for selling his shares and securing

NFR Communications as his first client in the rep firm he would start. By March, almost exactly four years after we bought the company, Bob sold his half to me. He also got a four-year contract to continue representing *Northwestern Financial Review* for ad sales. I viewed this as a pretty good way for me to dissolve this partnership peaceably. How often do you hear of partnerships ending up in court? I felt fortunate that this one ended with us still being friends.

Our client/company relationship, however, got off to a poor start when a dispute arose over Bob's commissions on ad sales. We eventually worked it out but it was a bad omen that foreshadowed a number of disputes over commissions. Questions always arose over which advertisers he truly serviced and which ones I serviced. I grew uncomfortable with the increasingly strained relationship but Bob had a contract and I was stuck.

Then a very strange, unexpected thing happened. At the end of 1997, Bob asked me to meet with him over breakfast at a Bloomington hotel. Between cups of coffee, he told me that he was feeling "called to do something new with his life," and he was interested in terminating our contract. The comment shocked me but I gladly agreed to accommodate. I personally felt the contract arrangement was going so badly that I was contemplating offering him some kind of buyout. The only thing Bob wanted was a check for the remainder of the money on the purchase of his stock, which I readily agreed to provide. On January 1, 1998, Bob terminated his contract with NFR Communications. I was the sole owner with no strings attached. I was now captain of my own ship, ready to sail solo.

✳ ✳ ✳

About that time, I set out to launch a new general business periodical. My feeling was that the existing such publications in the Twin Cities were missing a lot of good stories and NFR Communications could do better. I knew it was a long shot but I didn't care. So often throughout my life people had underestimated me, or encouraged me to take the easy way out as if that was all I was good for. Even as a kid my hockey coach told me to go out for goalie so I wouldn't have to skate so much. My counselor at the U of M told me to take freshman composition where we both knew I'd get an A, instead of a more challenging course where I would learn something I didn't already know. Now I owned my own business and I could do anything I pleased. No one could tell me my project was unrealistic. No one could tell me I should tackle something easier.

The first issue of the new publication would come out in September. We would mail it free to 40,000 small and medium-size businesses in the Twin Cities every other month, with all of the revenue coming from advertisers. I would serve as editor with most of the articles generated by freelance writers and existing *Northwestern Financial Review* staff. I recently had hired an assistant to work on a public relations project that never panned out, so we already had an outgoing personality on staff to help me with advertising sales. We would develop a prototype and media kit, and begin approaching potential advertisers by April 1. The budget for each issue was around $20,000. The staff was enthusiastic. Jackie Hilgert, our designer, even came up with a name for it: *Minnesota's Business Ink.*

I had no need of market research, focus group feedback, survey information nor advice from consultants. I could feel this product in my bones and I knew it would succeed. Sure we were understaffed and had only limited resources but I was convinced we'd build support as we got out and told potential advertisers what we were doing.

Between April and July, my sales assistant and I approached some 300 businesses about advertising. At $2,000 per page, we only needed 10 pages of advertising to make the project break-even, a goal I believed was attainable. Most of the business owners and managers expressed interest upon initial contact. "Sounds like a good opportunity," they'd say. "Send me a media kit." We sent out hundreds of kits.

In the meantime, I was lining up stories that would appear in the first issue. We scored big with a couple of stories involving recognizable area personalities. The front page would feature Rudy Boschwitz and family, which owned the Home Valu Stores, a chain of warehouse retail outlets that sold lumber, cabinets, tools and other staples of the home repair world. Boschwitz was a former U.S. Senator who granted us a lengthy interview. In addition, I developed a story about Bill Cooper, the quotable chief executive officer of TCF Financial, the third-largest bank in the state. Cooper was a straight-talking character who was chairing the state's Republican Party. We had good color photos to accompany each story.

The advertising commitments trickled in. We noted the progress on a large thermometer we posted in our production area. The top of the picture represented $20,000. By mid-July, we had about one-fifth of the thermometer colored red. I leveraged relationships from *Northwestern Financial Review* and got three community banks to advertise with us. A computer company we worked with also advertised. In mid-August we got our biggest commitment. First Bank agreed to buy a full-page, four-color advertisement in each of the first two issues. The bank was promoting its corporate credit card, which it felt would be attractive to the audience of small business owners and managers we would be reaching.

Then I got a phone call from the Minneapolis *Star Tribune*. A reporter, who had heard rumors about the impending launch, wanted to know more about *Business Ink*. I gave her an interview and she wrote a story about us that appeared in the Sunday edition of the newspaper, days before our first issue would be distributed. Things couldn't have been going better.

The premier edition of *Minnesota's Business Ink* was going to be a thing of beauty. Jackie took two dozen articles and laid them out in a reader-friendly format that filled 28 pages of newsprint. We put color on the covers and the center spread, maximizing the efficiency of the web press we used. The design challenge was significant because the publication had to be folded sufficiently to accommodate complicated postal regulations and still be interesting enough to attract potential newsstand customers. Jackie pulled it off. I felt certain that once area stores and businesses saw our first edition, they would be breaking down our door to buy advertising space in subsequent editions.

I looked around me at the office and declared, "I never thought I'd have all this!" The business was humming, we were doing new things, and we were about to launch something big. I loved my staff that was making all this happen. I looked at Jackie, the hardest worker of all, and wondered. Could she help me make the most of this business? Jackie was my best employee, by far. She worked smart and she invested herself in the company's efforts. When she took on a project, she didn't worry about the time clock or whether the task conformed to her job description. She just did it, and usually she did it well. She was an employer's dream and I began to think that maybe she could be my business partner. Cronin had made me nervous about partnerships, but I couldn't deny the fact that if I wanted to grow NFR Communications, I would need a partner. A person reaches a certain point of capacity where he simply cannot take on any more. My dad reached that point and decided to hold his business there. Did I want to limit the size of my business to that point? I really didn't know, and it made me anxious.

And Jackie's a woman. What kind of dynamic takes place between a man and a woman in the workplace? Can a married man and a married woman share a business partnership and corresponding friendship? Of course they can, I told myself. But what if he also thinks she's beautiful? I spent a lot of time asking peers if they thought a man and a woman could be friends. Could they create together without growing too close to one another? Most said no. "Sex will always get in the way," my printer told me. The radio psychologist I listened to on the way to work each morning said male/ female friendships outside marriage only lead to trouble.

As the publishing date for the first issue of *Busi-*

ness Ink approached, my anxiety expanded to include the possibility of failure. The first edition generated only $7,000 in advertising sales – small considering all the work we had put into our marketing effort. Worse, things didn't look much better for the second edition. All those media kits we sent out failed to generate the response we needed to make this publication viable. "We don't advertise with start-up publications," companies typically told us. "Call us after you've been in business for a year." I didn't have a year.

The day the first issue hit the streets, First Bank called.

"I can't believe you ran our ad opposite the jump for a story about TCF. They're a competitor!" an angry media buyer hollered into the phone.

The First Bank advertisement ran across from the TCF story, which carried a four-color picture. By placing the photo and ad on the same spread, we saved money on printing. "You're advertising a corporate product," I explained. "TCF is a retail bank. You two don't compete at all. And you didn't give us any position instructions with your ad."

"Of course we don't want to be anywhere near the competition. We are NOT paying for this ad and you can forget about running us in your next issue." My ear stung with the sharp sound of the phone slamming onto the receiver.

Then my sales assistant walked into my office. She closed the door and sat down on the other side of my desk, handing me a memo outlining an assertion that she deserved a bonus for her work during the past year. Boldly, she made it clear that she would quit if she didn't get what she wanted. I didn't see it her way. We had accomplished little, if anything, during the last year in terms of new ad sales. "I appreciate your work, and I encourage you to continue your efforts here," I said, "but a bonus at this time is out of the question."

She stared at me for what seemed like 10 minutes. Then she got up and walked out the door. She quit the next week.

As we approached the middle of October, I knew I was in over my head. Ad sales for the second issue were even lower than they had been for the first issue. Working with freelance writers proved more difficult than I expected. The quality of the copy failed to meet my expectations but because I was so pressed for time, I accepted most of it. I knew we would never win new advertisers with an inferior product. We would need to hire an editor and perhaps a reporter. Plus, the sales job was simply too big for one person. I'd have to bring on another salesperson. But what a gamble! They'd have to sell an awful lot of advertising to cover their salary and contribute to the company's bottom line. It seemed like a bad bet. I thought about Robert Hadland, the Lamberton, Minnesota, banker who'd succumbed to bankruptcy.

By November 1, it was over. Although the entire second edition was ready to go to press, I decided to scrap it. Printing and distributing the November *Busi-*

ness Ink would have meant another $13,000 loss. I wasn't prepared to handle that. Nor could I afford to put up with losses on subsequent issues.

I maintain that *Business Ink* was a reasonable concept but it needed a far bigger initial investment than I could afford. The venture was a little like a big airplane that needs 8,000 feet of runway; I could only give it 1,500 feet so it never got off the ground. I tried to look into the faces of my colleagues after sharing my decision. Their reaction was difficult to read, as most looked away from me. Only Jackie looked me in the eye. I could see her disappointment. Within the next few weeks, one of our writers and an administrative assistant quit. They found work with companies that perhaps held brighter prospects than NFR Communications. I wished them luck, something they apparently thought I had run out of.

I consider my *Business Ink* experience to be my graduate level business education. Costing about the same as an MBA, the venture taught me a lot about publishing, marketing, advertising, staff management, editorial development, and public relations. And I learned another thing – something my printer didn't understand. A man and a woman can be friends. Jackie stuck with me through the hard times when it would have been so easy to bail out. That meant a lot to me and I tried to think of ways to express appreciation. The next summer, I invited Jackie and her husband to spend a weekend up north with Susan and me. We vacationed at Breezy Point, a resort where we rented side-by-side condos on the beach of Pelican Lake. We had a great time fishing, picnicking, and telling stories around a campfire. It wasn't much, but then, in any friendship, it's the little things that count.

7

Lab Work

About a year after we were married, Susan and I wanted to start a family but we had trouble conceiving. A few times Susan said she felt sure she was pregnant but then her period would come and our hopes would be dashed. Susan's disappointment was huge. I was disappointed too but not quite as dejected. For years, Susan had fantasized about being a mother; now that dream was in jeopardy. I dreamed about being a father, but I had other dreams too — like being a big-name publisher and a business success. With the distraction of professional pursuits, I found it possible to hold onto the dream of recreating the family I grew up in. In the back of my mind, I truly believed we would become pregnant.

But we didn't. The more time that went by, the more I thought about those science classes in high school where my experiments never seemed to work. The teacher would demonstrate the volcanic result of mixing certain chemicals according to a protocol. Inviting us to copy him, I would do exactly as I thought I was supposed to do and my test tube never responded … no change in color, no smell, nothing. I would ask the teacher why and he would just say, "you must have done it wrong." I knew I didn't. In the end, there just wasn't any explanation. Twenty years later, I'm apparently still not getting the chemistry right. And there's still no explanation.

We sought medical help but after dozens of doctor appointments, no answers emerged. The doctors poked and prodded our bodies repeatedly but never came up with anything that made sense. They told Susan she might have endometriosis. They told me I had low sperm motility. Both conditions could reduce our chances of getting pregnant but neither should have made it impossible.

A man doesn't like to be told he is infertile, that his sperm is somehow not good enough, that his body fluids are benign. A man likes to think of his semen as strong stuff, life-giving juice that could be dangerous if used incorrectly. A man likes to feel that he could impregnate an oak tree if he had to. Getting a woman pregnant was supposed to be a no-brainer, especially a woman he truly loves. I was being told I couldn't and it was beginning to tick me off. Wasn't infertility for people who had smoked marijuana, or for people who drank too much? Wasn't it for people with blood disorders, or for people who worked near nuclear power plants? We weren't supposed to be infertile. We were healthy and strong – we didn't even smoke. We wanted kids. We understood the cycles of our bodies. We understood the science that allowed us to pinpoint the exact days of peak fertility.

But it wasn't working. Was it the sex? Was I somehow not doing it right? Did it matter who was on top? Did we need to allow a certain amount of time between tries? We contemplated everything.

I worried about what people would think of us. Surely they would misjudge us, calling us DINKs for "Dual Income, No Kids." Everyone would think we were doing this on purpose, not having kids. They might question our faith, saying "they're Catholic but they don't have any kids."

What were we to do with our state of childlessness? We took trips to Europe, ate out a lot, and did things that only childless couples can do. We went to the movie theater several nights in a row, got away almost every weekend, and took time for jogging and aerobics. But none of it satisfied. I wanted to bounce a kid on my knee. I wanted to play on the floor with my baby. I wanted to teach someone the alphabet and build imaginary cities with blocks. I was also scared to death of dying alone. I didn't want to become like Leo in Saranac Lake. I wanted to have a lot of kids to pass my knowledge on to. I dreamed of telling stories to children on my lap but it didn't look like I would get that chance. After three years of trying to get pregnant with no success, my dreams seemed shattered. Susan grew unhappy, which became particularly obvious whenever a friend or relative announced they were pregnant.

Despite the facts, I denied we were infertile. I just couldn't believe it. Nearly 800,000 Catholics live in the archdiocese of St. Paul and Minneapolis and perhaps only a few of us respect the Church's teaching on birth control. Not only did we respect it, but Susan and I were among those who tried to help people live it. How could we continue to promote natural family planning if we had no reason to practice it? What right did I have to tell married couples they should periodically abstain when that restriction didn't apply to me? All the credibility behind the presentation Susan and I had delivered before hundreds of people over the years was gone. Why us, God? What were we supposed to do now?

❋ ❋ ❋

The process of diagnosing my fertility situation was long and strung out. When I first agreed with Susan to see a doctor, I really only anticipated a single meeting. I figured he could look me over, take an X-ray or EKG, and figure the whole thing out. But he couldn't. In fact, it was a process of trial and error, and the "trials" were not very sophisticated. The doctor did a lot of listening with his stethoscope. First he listened to various places on my chest and back. I couldn't see what this could have to do with fertility but I didn't ask questions. Then he listened to my groin and testicles. The cold stainless steal surface of the instrument felt like ice cubes. I wondered what he was listening for. What were my testicles supposed to sound like? Then he hooked up some kind of amplifying device to the stethoscope. A box with several knobs and dials, something akin to a transistor radio, broadcast static that meant nothing to me. The doctor took notes on a clipboard as he listened.

Other forms of poking and prodding followed, including those that I was warned would cause "temporary discomfort." It all seemed remarkably crude to me. Surely there was some diagnostic machine that could pinpoint my trouble and suggest a remedy. They have such machines for cars, why not people? The engine on your 1999 Chevy running a little rough? A mechanic attaches a computer to the vehicle and within minutes he can tell you exactly what's wrong, the make of the engine's spark plugs, your optimum gas mileage, and probably the weather in Tibet. It's got to be a lot easier being an automobile than a human being, especially one that isn't working just right.

Every time I went to the doctor, they asked for a semen sample. "Here," the female assistant said, handing me a cup. "When you've got a sample, come on out." She pointed me toward a room with an easy chair, no windows, and girlie magazines on a table. I couldn't believe modern medicine would put me in such a quandary. I didn't want to masturbate into that cup. I knew it was immoral but how fair was it that I was infertile? I wanted kids, after all. Wouldn't God look the other way? I looked at the cover of one of the magazines and began to stare at the girl's eyes. They were blue and inviting.

I recalled the first time I looked through a pornographic magazine. I was in the throes of puberty. Mark Hillendbrand and I were walking through the alley when we saw a garbage can where someone was throwing away a collection of *Playboy* and *Penthouse* magazines! There had to be 100 of them. We wanted to look at those pictures but we couldn't just sit down and start flipping through the pages; we needed some sort of plan. So we found a cardboard box and taped a false bottom in it about three-fourths of the way up. Mark's mom was sitting in the kitchen, directly on the route between the back door and Mark's room. We would have to get by her undetected. We exited the house with the box, telling her someone was throwing away a bunch of tennis balls and we were going to get them. We went through the garage where we filled the top of our box with old tennis balls, leaving three-fourths of the box empty for our secret treasure. We bolted down the block and loaded the magazines in through the bottom of the box, re-sealing with packing tape. We returned through the back door of Mark's house. Mark's mom was there. The box I was holding looked to be filled with tennis balls. "Look at all the tennis balls," Mark said. "We're going to take them to my room and count them." I didn't say a word. I was glad it wasn't me who had to lie.

We got the package to Mark's room, removed the tape from the bottom of the box and let the smutty magazines spill onto Mark's bed. We spent the next three hours studying our find, covering our suspicious silence by playing records from the rock band *Chicago* on Mark's stereo. There was a lot to see. Most of it was new to me. It seemed like the perfect crime.

The next day, Mark told me his mom discovered the magazines and made him throw them all away – after ripping each one to shreds.

That's what I wanted to do with the magazines they offered me in that little room at the clinic. I looked at the girl's mouth, her glossy lips parted. A bit of her tongue was showing between her pearly teeth. How does the camera capture seduction so perfectly? It's a hell of a trick. And I hate the people who do it. They tricked me. I thought beautiful Becky really did like beaches and haylofts but now I see that was all a lie. This little room at the fertility clinic exposed the cheese-cake for what it was – a masturbatory aid. There was nothing real-life about those pictures I pored over in Mark's room. Hefner, Guccione, they ruined the mystery of life for me. You know what the Bible says about a person who steals the innocence of a child – better that he be thrown into the sea with a rock tied around his neck! It's like the man who tells you the surprise ending of a novel before you even get a chance to pick up the book and read it. He's ruined it for you. There's no way you can enjoy the story the way the author intended. The whole thing makes me sick. Modern medicine was going to help us conceive and the best they could come up with was pornography. I emerged from the little room at the clinic. I handed the lady my sample without looking at her. I hate this. I'm not doing this again, ever.

And yet other requests for semen samples came; I told them I would bring my sample from home. "Fine, but it can't be more than 45 minutes old," I was told.

The Couple to Couple League offered advice in one of its publications to people facing the moral dilemma we faced: how to provide a semen sample and still respect our faith which asks us not to masturbate. The book explained that you could collect the semen by having sex while wearing a condom. We'd have to poke holes in the condom before use, however, to allow some of the sperm through so pregnancy remained possible. The advice seemed reasonable to Susan and me.

The first step was a trip to Walgreen's. I didn't go to the one in my neighborhood but to one a few miles away. I wandered up and down the aisles, lingering at the birthday cards and cough medicines. I didn't really want people to know why I was there, even if all the people around were complete strangers.

I am not naive. I am an adult with a college degree. I have interviewed U.S. senators and the presidents of billion-dollar corporations. But all of a sudden in this drug store I felt like a pimply-faced teenager. I didn't know anything about condoms. The schools I attended didn't teach me about things like that. I found the condom display and everything was new to me. Gosh, there were a lot of choices! Who were the geniuses who devised condoms in a variety of textures and flavors? Who were the marketing guys who came up with names like "Trojan" and "Magnum?" Why were some condoms scented like bananas and strawberries? I picked the most benign offering and headed for the check-out counter, stopping along the way to pick up a pack of gum, a *Field &Stream* magazine, and a couple of blank cassette tapes for the VCR. I reached into my wallet only to discover I didn't have any money. My wallet was empty! And I didn't have enough change in my pockets to cover a $12 purchase. Blast! I had to use a credit card. I made eye contact with the person behind the counter. Staring back at me with vacant eyes, the clerk certainly didn't care what I was buying. So why should I have been nervous? But I was. I rendered my plastic, signed the sales slip and bolted out of there, feeling uneasy about my signature having confirmed the purchase of a birth control device.

In the middle of the day, when the traffic was light, it took about 25 minutes to drive from our house in south Minneapolis to the fertility clinic, which was near downtown St. Paul. It seemed reasonable that we could collect our sample, get dressed, get in the car and drive to St. Paul, park the car and deliver the sample in the allotted 45 minutes. In any event, we considered it to be preferable to producing the sample by myself in a weird little room at the clinic.

Susan and I had talked about this for weeks, devising all kinds of ways to shave seconds off of our delivery time. As it was winter, the car would have to be warmed up ahead of time. We could each keep our socks on while we made love as to reduce the time needed to dress. We would lay out our clothes ahead of time. At bedside, I would keep a collection jar and a towel, which we would wrap around the jar to insulate the sample from the cold.

And, of course, I would have to know how to use a condom. The box came with instructions, obviously prepared for someone educated no further than the 10th grade. Most of the information was communicated through simple drawings. The written part was sparse, and I was offended that they used the word "prick" to refer to my sex organ.

When the day of my 10 a.m. appointment came, we got everything ready. I had arranged to take the morning off from work. Susan and I sat side by side on the bed, naked except for our socks, and poked holes in a condom with a pushpin we had sterilized with a match. "We need more holes," I said. "No, we need a good sample," Susan protested. We poked a dozen holes in the prophylactic device, none of them visible.

Emerging Son

Not long after we began to caress, I became aroused and I had to interrupt everything to put on the rubber. This little break took a lot of the steam out of our interaction but it wasn't long before I had my sample. Immediately after climaxing, we separated and I sat up to remove the condom. The clock was now ticking. Everything I did from that point on seemed to be happening in slow motion. It seemed impossible that we would beat the time limit. I transferred the sample to the jar, wrapped it in a towel, washed, dressed, and ran to the car. Susan had beaten me there and was waiting in the driver's seat. The roads were slippery and the traffic was slow, so we barely made it to the clinic on time. Susan dropped me off at the front door so I could deliver the goods while she parked the car. By the time I handed off the jar, we only had a few minutes to spare.

In a couple of weeks I had another appointment and the doctors wanted another sample. With each sample, they were discovering a problem with the sperm. Only a small percentage of them were sufficiently active to make it to the fallopian tube where one of the sperm was suppose to fertilize an ovum and start a new life. Several samples were needed to verify that the condition was chronic. They told me my one-time results could be an aberration due to stress or other factor.

When we considered how closely we had run up against the clock during our last sample collection, we decided we needed a new plan. Not far from the fertility clinic was a building called the Civic Center Hotel, budget lodging designed mostly for the fans who came to St. Paul to watch their team compete in the state high school tournaments. The halls in the hotel were illuminated with lights that couldn't possibly have consumed more than 40 watts of electrical power. But the surroundings didn't matter to Susan and me; proximity to the fertility clinic was everything. We knew we could use a room there and walk over to the clinic in 10 minutes, even on a snowy day. So when the next appointment came, which was scheduled for late afternoon, we went to the Civic Center Hotel and checked in.

It felt funny to check into a hotel without any luggage. I couldn't get the song "Mrs. Robinson" out of my head as we ascended in a dingy elevator. The room was adequate for our purpose – it had a bed. We never disturbed the curtains, opened the closet, or turned the television set on during our stay, which lasted less than an hour. Nothing about the room would stimulate a romantic mood; we'd have to create that on our own. And we did, so that within a half hour of checking in we had our sample. We dressed and walked out, leaving the key and the unmade bed in our wake. I was a little unsettled at the idea that anyone watching us would misinterpret what we were doing. Surely we weren't the only ones to have ever paid $55 for a half-hour's use of a hotel room.

Emerging Son

Susan and I walked out through the lobby. I carried a brown grocery bag by the handles; inside was the sample jar wrapped in a towel. I nodded at the teenage check-in clerk at the registration desk; I'd never see her again, nor would I want to. She would only be a reminder of the serious problem I was finally beginning to accept. My sperm really wasn't much good. I wouldn't be able to get my wife pregnant. I wouldn't be able to give my wife what she really wanted – children, motherhood, the experience of pregnancy and childbirth. Her hips would never part to make way for the passage of a new person. Her breasts would never swell with the nourishment a newborn needs. I would never get to put my hand on her belly and feel a kicking baby. I would never get to raise a kid who looks like me. If I never saw that hotel clerk again, the situation would be a little easier to deny.

* * *

After several clinic visits, my doctor finally recommended action. He said I had a varicocele, which is a collection of dilated veins in the scrotum. The condition was caused by leaking valves in the testicular veins, which drain blood away from the testes. The doctor said the blood was pooling and raising my internal temperature. The warmer climate was affecting the sperm. He called the condition common and said with a simple surgery he could tie off the swollen veins, which would stop the pooling of blood. The temperature in my testes would drop to normal and the sperm would regain their normal motility.

For an experienced urologist, the surgery was a piece of cake. He could perform the procedure with one hand tied behind his back, but for me it may as well have been a quadruple bypass. Hospitals, clinics, doctors, injections, and medical procedures make me uneasy. Call me squeamish. The idea of deliberately cutting through my skin completely repulses me. So why is it the first time I need surgery it involves my scrotum? I can't even listen to a guy tell me about his vasectomy without crossing my legs.

That summer, Susan and I traveled to Grand Rapids, Michigan, to attend the international convention of the Couple to Couple League, a once-every-two-years event that attracted about 500 families from all over the country. The four-day conference featured presentations with titles such as "The Effects of Contraception on Popular Morality," "Sexual Dilemmas Made Easy" and "How to Promote Natural Family Planning in a Secular World." Our first convention, we felt somehow conspicuous by our lack of children. The CCL convention was definitely a family fest where kids were entertained while the parents listened to speakers. Even the main events were modified to accommodate mothers who might have to care for very young children. Speeches were piped into special rooms via closed circuit television for mothers who needed to nurse their children, and adults were encouraged after presentations to wave their arms in the air instead of clapping so that children sleeping on mom's lap wouldn't be awakened.

The children were everywhere – running, laughing, and playing. These children were like the ones in the family I grew up in. And all I wanted was another family like that. I had played it straight, done all the right things. I didn't sleep around as a single guy. I loved my wife. I went to church and believed in God. I set aside my own fantasies about marriage being a nonstop sexual free-for-all and accepted natural family planning. I was surrounded by couples for whom this formula worked. But it wasn't working for Susan and me. Why not? Was I proud and arrogant? Was this God putting me in my place? Did I need to take better care of myself – lower my cholesterol or build my upper body strength? Or was I just trying to find reasons where there were none — fairness when no one ever promised the world is a fair place?

Susan and I went for a walk between speeches. The campus of Calvin College in Grand Rapids was beautiful. The sky was blue, the sun was bright, and the foliage was full. Everything looked so fertile.

"Will you do the surgery?" Susan asked.

"It makes me a little nervous."

"What makes you nervous about it?"

"The part where they cut into my groin."

"What choice do we have?" she asked.

Lab Work

The fact was there were a lot of choices. We could have gone childless. We could have considered adoption. We could have kept on trying to conceive.

I remembered the advice my dad gave me on our wedding day.

"I guess we don't have a choice." I said. "I'll do the surgery."

* * *

The surgery was set for mid-January 1993. It would begin at 7:00 in the morning, so I had to be at the hospital by 6:00. It was a 20-minute procedure but I would need four to five hours of recovery time. The goal was to get me out of the surgery center by mid afternoon. I was told I'd be walking around within three days as if nothing had happened. Susan drove me to the hospital on the appointed day. She parked herself in the waiting room with an *Ellery Queen* mystery magazine, which would occupy her until I was ready to go home. I kissed Susan on the lips and told her I loved her.

After changing into a gown they gave me, I lay on my back on a table. They asked me to stretch my arms out perpendicular to my body and they secured my wrists with Velcro straps. They injected an intravenous needle into the middle of my left forearm and all I could think of were Roman soldiers pounding big metal spikes into the hands of Jesus, not the all-powerful Son of God, but the unjustly persecuted carpenter. Once the needle was in, they asked me to count backward from 100. I recall getting as far as 97.

I woke up three-and-a-half hours later in a recovery room with Susan at my side. She gave me all of her attention and I was grateful for a loving wife. I wanted to tell her everything that happened but I had no recollection of anything. I looked under my gown and discovered that a surgery had, in fact, taken place. My mouth tasted like rubber and I was told later they had inserted a tube down my throat, something that apparently was common during surgery. Within a few hours, my head cleared and my confidence returned. I was ready to go home. They wheeled me as far as the hospital's front door and Susan helped me get into the passenger side of the front seat of our car.

"Tom," Susan said. "I love you more than ever."

"What? Why?"

"You went under the knife. I know how you hate medical things. I know you dreaded this surgery. You did this for us, and I love you for it," she said.

"I love you too," I said.

* * *

A follow-up visit to the fertility doctor, however, exposed the surgery to be a failure. The urologist pressed his cold stethoscope to my testicle and heard something he didn't like. One moment he was admiring the shape of the incision and the next moment he was declaring the surgery "a disaster."

"This didn't work at all. The blood is still pooling. You can hear it," he said. He let me listen, although I couldn't make any sense out of the noise.

The following fall I had the surgery again and this time it was a success. Upon listening to my testicles during the follow-up visit, the doctor heard nothing, which was good — the blood was not pooling. There would be nothing to cause an elevated temperature where the sperm were being produced; all my sperm should be normally active. Surely at least one sperm would be able to make it into the fallopian tube for a fateful encounter with an ovum.

With a renewed sense of hope, Susan and I went at it. We made love every night for three months; sometimes we even made love on my lunch hour.

But nothing happened. All our efforts were fruitless.

Starting another round of clinic visits, tests showed motility remained low. Only about 10 percent of the sperm were active, far too few to achieve conception. The surgeries had accomplished nothing.

Two options were presented. We could pursue artificial insemination, which meant they could take some of the active sperm from a sample and mechanically place them next to an ovum inside Susan. The other option was to ingest a particular kind of steroid. This would increase sperm production sufficiently to get enough active ones to make conception possible.

The steroid treatment, however, had side effects. "About a quarter of the men who use this suffer severe hip bone degeneration," a doctor told us.

Susan and I were asked to choose between a procedure we consider to be immoral and one that may require me to undergo hip replacement surgery by the time I turn 45. We decided against both of them and turned our attention to adoption.

8

Waiting

A stack of half-completed forms, government documents, and other papers sat on our kitchen counter for weeks as we waded through the process of adopting a child. I looked at the unkempt pile of papers and sighed, beginning to believe we would never get "the call." We were waiting for the day when the social services agency would call us to say they had a child for us. We had been waiting for months and it got Susan and me down. Family, which apparently came easy to my mom and dad, seemed elusive as I stared at the pile of dog-eared paperwork.

Initially, Susan and I figured we'd adopt a baby from Minnesota but we dropped that idea, learning it could take years. I was already 33 and Susan was pushing 30 – my parents had nearly all their kids by the time they were my age. We didn't have years to build a family. We wanted several kids and the snail's pace with which the domestic adoption process progressed made it unlikely that we could complete more than a couple of adoptions in a decade or so.

We turned our attention to international adoption but timing was only part of the reason. I was unsure about the open process that's the standard for adoptions in the United States. In typical domestic adoptions, couples like Susan and me list their names in a "waiting families" book maintained by one of the social services agencies. The listing includes personal information such as family history, interests, household life, religious convictions, and educational background. A prospective couple might even include a photograph. Interested pregnant women scan the books and pick out a few couples they like, then the social services agency sets up meetings between the selected couples and the birth mother.

After the interviews, the birth mother selects a couple for the child. If she follows through with the adoption, the child joins the new adoptive parents, although the law gives a birth mother a number of weeks to change her mind. During the interviews, birth mothers usually request the opportunity to maintain contact with the child. Some only want to see an updated photograph every year, while others want monthly visits or more. Adoptive parents willing to accept greater levels of birth mother contact have the best chance of being selected.

This isn't at all what I had in mind as I thought about the family I wanted. Open adoption could only be confusing for the child, I told myself, and I sensed it might be frustrating for me. What if the birth parents tell the kid something I don't agree with? Who would the kid listen to — me or the birth mom? I didn't want any part of that kind of dilemma. Ultimately, the open adoption process seemed to be no better than applying for a job in a bad economy – send in a resume, wait to be contacted, come in for an interview and accept whatever arrangement was offered. Only by adopting a child from another country could we avoid the potential pitfalls I saw in the open adoption process.

We enlisted the aid of Lutheran Social Services, which was known for its international adoption programs. It wasn't particularly important to us which country the children would come from. We only knew that we wanted to adopt more than one child over time and we figured it would be easier if all our children came from the same country. LSS introduced us to an adoption program it shared with Colombia, a country with a long history of accepting adoptive parents from Minnesota. Although ignorant of Latin American culture and unable to speak more than a dozen words of Spanish, we signed up.

We had only one criterion: we wanted a healthy child. Was that selfish? A couple that conceives a child doesn't get to stipulate it will only accept a healthy child. Adoptive couples, however, can make such a choice and we were making the most of our situation. What fertile couple wouldn't ask for a healthy child if they had the opportunity? I talked through the logic in my head but still felt a little guilty. I wondered whether we weren't just rich folks who came up with a way to buy ourselves out of a problem. I mean, not everyone can travel to another continent to adopt a child without interference from birth parents. But I had no delusions about what we were doing. We weren't adopting to be heroes. I just wanted a healthy, traditional family like the one I grew up in.

✳ ✳ ✳

Susan and I hated the waiting, which seemed as fruitless as our efforts to conceive. Emotionally, the process drained us, but intellectually we knew a referral would be coming. A child would be placed with us at some point. When we initiated the adoption process in early 1994, we hoped to get a child and be back in our home as a family of three by Christmas. Susan called LSS about every other week during that summer. "Any news yet?" she'd ask. The answer was always the same, "no." We wondered, what was the hold up? What could possibly be delaying the process? We never got a satisfactory answer, which just made the waiting all the more difficult.

Although it was an anxious time, we also knew we were about to lose a period in our lives that was special unto itself. Married for five years, Susan and I spent so much uninterrupted time together — time to focus on each other and do what we wanted, when we wanted. We were grateful and as we thought ahead, we kept thinking *this might be the last time that ...*   Every time we went out for a meal at a restaurant we thought "This will be the last time we will be able to do this for a while," understanding that a baby would become a priority far ahead of a night out. Oh sure, we'd probably still go out after getting a child, but it would not be on the worry-free basis that we enjoyed then.

In spring of 1994 Susan and I decided to make the most of our soon-to-end freedom and traveled to Rome to see Pope John Paul II, whom we considered to be one of the greatest people of our era. A man of courage, John Paul II had written so much about the issues that Susan and I faced in our efforts to start a family. He certainly wasn't trying to win any popularity contests, speaking out against artificial ways to conceive. And long before we knew we had fertility problems, we contemplated his words on chastity: he promoted it for all unmarried people and he even dared to say it had a role in marriage. His reasoning, which made sense to Susan and me, was so counter-cultural we believed it had to be guided by a force beyond this earth.

We lived in a time when we could go see the Pope — the successor to Peter in an unbroken line of Church leadership — even if we lived halfway around the world. We had some money saved up. This was the time to go.

The Pope conducted a public blessing on Sundays,

and he hosted a general audience on Wednesdays. We wanted to get in on both. Before leaving for Rome that March, we contacted the local archdiocesan office to ask about the Wednesday audience. They contacted someone in Rome and told us where to pick up tickets once we arrived.

Following an overnight plane ride, Susan and I explored the Eternal City and it seemed like a dream. Rome is not Minneapolis. The streets were chaotic, the buildings were centuries old, and there were monuments everywhere. We saw the Colosseum, the Trevi fountain and the Spanish Steps where crowds of young folks congregated. Italians seemed to have all day to sit around and talk. The sidewalk cafes were perpetually crowded with people drinking coffee. Susan and I shared a cappuccino at one restaurant in front of the Pantheon.

"Susan," I asked between sips. "Do you love me?"

"Of course," she said. "What do you ask that for?"

"I know this isn't exactly what you signed up for."

"What do you mean?" she asked.

"You wanted a husband who could father your child, and you ended up with me," I said.

"Oh, Tom, stop that."

"You're too nice to admit that it is an issue," I said. "And maybe it's not an issue for you, but I am still working through it."

"Tom, I love you. You are who you are, and I love you."

Waiting

We had had this conversation a number of times before. Sometimes it takes a while for a man to accept who he is.

✳ ✳ ✳

A friend had given us a tip about a tour into the bowels of St. Peter's Cathedral. Outside the church, we approached one of the Swiss guards, identifiable by a brightly colored uniform, and asked about the "scavi tour." *Scavi* is the Italian word for "excavation," and we found this to be a descriptive word for the tour, which took us into caves below the Cathedral. We descended deep underground with a small group of tourists led by a seminarian from Wisconsin. He told us that most of the rooms we were seeing were mausoleums and graveyards that dated back to the third and fourth centuries. Roman Christians gathered for Mass here during those first centuries when public allegiance to the faith could mean death. That Colosseum we marveled at earlier in the trip was the site of persecution when Christians were commonly thrown to the lions.

Well into the tour, we found ourselves staring at a grave protected by a see-through case. Buried here was St. Peter, killed by Roman soldiers in the first century, crucified upside down. Somewhere, nearly a quarter of a mile above us, a statue of St. Peter welcomed people to the enormous plaza in front of the

Cathedral. There, Peter is depicted holding a set of keys — the "keys to the kingdom" given to him by Christ Himself — as described in the sixteenth chapter of Matthew's gospel. And here, his remains lay before us. The seminarian explained that we were located directly under the high altar of the Cathedral. Scripture says: "Peter, you are rock and upon this rock I will build my church." The proximity of Peter's grave in relation to the Cathedral added another layer of meaning to that scripture verse, which is absolutely central to the Catholic faith.

✳ ✳ ✳

Susan and I arrived at St. Peter's Square about 8:30 on Wednesday morning for the 11 o'clock audience with the Pope. By then, a long line of people was already waiting to get into the hall that was specially constructed for these weekly programs. Our tickets got us in the door but it was all general seating once inside. The same person who tipped us off about the scavi tour, told us we should try to get a seat near an aisle because after the program the Pope walks around the audience and shakes hands. Perhaps everyone else with a ticket had gotten the same tip because once inside we saw that everyone was going for the aisle seats. We were lucky enough to sit just two seats away from the center aisle.

The audience hall featured a stage with an imposing copper-colored sculpture on the wall. There was a chair in front of it where the Pope sat. The hall holds 7,000 people and it was full the day we went. People came in groups, dressed to represent their home country. Short, brown-skinned nuns in habits waved. A group of young men and women in bright red-and-white peasant-style clothing sang. And black-skinned men and women in white, floor-length robes chanted. Many people, including me, held a camera.

The ceremony began with a greeting. The Pope said "hello" and "welcome" in more than two dozen languages. After each salutation, a group of people who apparently understood what was said stood up and cheered. The atmosphere seemed more like a football game than a religious service. The Pope preached, alternating between French, Italian, and English, although we were there more for the whole Papal experience than we were to listen to a sermon.

At the conclusion of his presentation, the Pope did, in fact, walk up and down the aisles to offer personal greet-ings. As he made his way down the center aisle nearer and nearer to where we were standing, Susan

stretched out her arm. A woman at the aisle stepped aside to make room for Susan at the barricade. I stayed in the background and readied my camera. John Paul II walked right in front of us, Susan coming to within inches of touching him. I got a good picture of the Pope, looking our way, Susan's hand visible in the lower periphery of the image.

We got what we came for: a live audience with our spiritual grand marshal, our five-star general in the war against sin, our leader in the universal campaign to love neighbor and foe. I was struck by how easy it was for us to get so close to the Pope, a world leader whose authority knows no political boundaries. The man who was guiding us into eternity was so much more accessible than any important political figure, whose impact on us would be so insignificant by comparison. If we ever got the kids Susan and I so deeply wanted, perhaps we'd name them John and Paul. Susan and I just looked at each other and breathed after the Pope was long past us. We had been to big events before but no rock concert, no athletic event, had ever left us feeling so drained. We were exhausted by the time we left the audience hall and feasted that afternoon on a low-cost but mountainous plate of spaghetti.

✳ ✳ ✳

Back home, the details of the adoption process were weighing us down. Before a couple could adopt, they had to prepare an information packet called a "home study." The packet required couples to describe everything in writing, from job history, to family status, to personal philosophies, to religion, to the television shows they enjoy. And a social worker conducted interviews.

"Are you angry about your fertility situation?" asked an expressionless social worker.

"No," I said. "I was sad about it but not angry."

"So you are in denial?" she responded, writing "denial" on a notebook she kept on her lap.

"I am not in denial!" I shouted.

The social worker underlined her original answer in the notebook.

LSS wanted to know so much about us before they would approve us for an adoption. We had to give them a picture of our extended family. A social worker came to our home. She looked in every room, humming as she checked things off her clipboard. "Will the child have her own room?" we were asked. "How old is the house? Is this lead-based paint? Are these pipes protected with asbestos? I see. How many smoke alarms do you have?"

Then they asked about our plans for discipline. "You won't be spanking the child will you?" I had to think fast. How was I supposed to answer? Truth was, I didn't know if I would be spanking our child or not. Of course I hoped I wouldn't ever have to. But could I imagine a situation where a swat on the bottom was the only way to get my kid's attention? Yes.

"No," I told the social worker.

LSS required couples considering international adoption to participate in a cross-cultural workshop, a three-hour meeting Susan and I dutifully attended with a dozen other couples. The session offered a potpourri of information about cultures around the world but there was little on Colombia and even less on some of the really important questions we had about adoption. Susan wanted to know about adoptive nursing and I wanted to know if there were any shortcuts we could take to minimize the paperwork demanded by the Colombian court system. The workshop didn't address those topics.

Instead, workshop leaders spent a lot of time describing the ramifications of inter-racial adoption. Our adoption would fall into this category, although I had a hard time considering Colombians as being a different race. Colombians have skin colors that vary as much as Americans – some are dark and others are light. One prospective adoptive couple shared concern that their relatives wouldn't accept their South American-born child as readily as they accepted their relatives born in the United States. "I know they will make an issue of the brown skin," the wife said. "I have relatives who refused to come to my baby shower."

Although a social worker told us these kinds of reactions were common, our relatives were supportive. In fact, Susan's parents were excited about the culture that Colombian children might bring to a clan that was otherwise dominated by Scandinavians. The social worker asked us to consider several questions: Would we celebrate Colombian holidays with our new child? Would we teach them Spanish? Would we teach the kids about Colombian history and culture? Would we make an effort to expose them to other Colombian children living in the Twin Cities? We listened to the questions and we sensed that some of the couples took the exercise quite seriously, but one couple didn't.

"The kid is going to be raised in Minnesota," said a woman. "We are going to raise an American. All this heritage stuff is nice but the kid won't be living in Colombia. He'll be living in Minnesota. He won't need to know how to speak Spanish. He is going to need to know how to speak English."

The social worker nodded.

We were eager to encourage our child to study his or her heritage, and to learn to speak Spanish. Francophiles since college, Susan and I were conversant in French, which did us no good at all in our current station in life. When we first began to think about international adoption, I was hoping there would be some orphanage in the south of France that would need an American couple to take a child. No such Mediterranean opportunity existed so we prepared to immerse ourselves in a culture that would be entirely new to us.

The prospective parents we talked to at the seminar seemed like well-educated people living upper-middle class lifestyles. Many were managers at Fortune 500 companies like 3M or Honeywell. As I thought about how the responsibility of parenthood would affect Susan and me, I looked around the room. Susan, who had worked the last two years at the magazine with me, gave up her job in anticipation of spending time at home with our new baby. How many of our peers intended to stay home full-time with their new child? Would they put their baby in daycare? Would nine hours a day at a KinderCare be much of an improvement over life in an orphanage? I wish the social worker had shed some light on this for me.

At one point, we needed to be fingerprinted by an official from the U.S. Immigration and Naturalization Service, which happened to have an office in the basement of a building in Bloomington. We got an appointment only after working an automated phone system for hours. One time, Susan called at 3:30 and was put on hold for 90 minutes. At 5 p.m. sharp, the line clicked to a dial tone.

The service wasn't any better in person. Spending more than an hour in a hot, crowded waiting room, we listened to the low-level chatter of people who sat around us. Much of the banter was in languages I didn't understand and I wondered why so many people were there. These were not prospective adoptive couples. Mostly, I guessed, they were foreigners looking for a legal way to stay in the United States. They must have been highly motivated because there was nothing welcoming about this INS office. In fact, our country seemed to be going out of its way to express indifference toward these people from a multitude of lands.

No one acknowledged us as we waited to be fingerprinted so the authorities could check us against their national database of criminals. Susan and I knew we weren't criminals but they made us feel like we were. Eventually our number came up and we paid a fee. An aide helped us roll each finger in ink and apply it to a special fingerprint card. We were told to relax. Tight finger muscles apparently don't provide a good print. We had to give two sets of prints so by the time we were finished, we were in desperate need of the industrial strength cleaning solution they offered us on our way out. Months later we received a computer-generated form from an office in Washington, D.C., telling us that our fingerprints had failed to turn up any matches in their criminal files. We could continue with the adoption process.

We also needed to have a psychological evaluation. We were given the name of a doctor, who interviewed us separately, asking us questions about our childhood and whether we were addicted to drugs or alcohol. Ultimately, he gave us each a certificate verifying our sanity. I joked that I was going to have it framed and hung in my office so that if anyone ever questioned my sanity, I could point to the certificate for proof. Susan reminded me that the certificate was dated and valid only for six months.

Emerging Son

I can understand the extensive vetting but I wondered why adoptive parents were held to a higher standard than birth parents. A couple gets pregnant, has a kid, and raises it any way they want. No one checks to see if their home is good enough. No one wants to see a picture of their relatives. No one asks how they plan to discipline their child. No, those questions are reserved for adoptive couples. I complained, not so much because I wanted anything to change but because I found the venting to be somewhat therapeutic.

※ ※ ※

About a year after initiating the adoption process, we got word from Bogotá that a little girl was waiting for us. Finally! We were ecstatic. The infant was living at *Ayudame*, a private orphanage in Colombia's capital city. That's all they told us, so we sped to the LSS office to look at a picture of her. I couldn't believe we were about to get a family started, something we had been working on for five years, something I had been thinking about for more than a decade.

The adoption secretary showed us the photo. It was a tiny color Polaroid, no bigger than a postage stamp. Susan looked at it first. I stared at the picture, arched between her fingers to minimize the glare. I had to squint to get a good look at it.

"Oh," was my first thought. "What big nostrils." Such a stupid reaction to a special moment. But no matter. Paula, the name given by her birth mother, was the most beautiful one-month-old baby I had ever seen. Her cheeks were plump; the top of her head featured a thick crop of black hair. The photo was framed tight, so we couldn't see what she was wearing. It didn't even show her neck, just a fleshy double chin. She had big, dark eyes that were looking straight at me. Her lips were pursed, like she was waiting for a kiss and I planted a big one right on the picture. And then I kissed Susan. We skipped back to the car, pausing once for Susan to turn a pirouette.

During the next couple of days as Susan and I prepared to go Bogotá to get our baby, we were as happy as could be. Susan and I would, at last, be parents. We'd actually have a family.

I hoped our new family would be as happy as I remembered my family being when I was a kid.

9

Gifts of the Andes

Colombia, a mesh of jungle, mountain, and ocean, welcomed us that spring of 1995. Flags — displaying "yellow for the riches of the land, blue for the oceans on two borders and red for the blood of the liberators" — flew everywhere in Santafe De Bogotá. Somewhere in this city of seven and a half million people a tiny orphanage housed a two-month-old baby who had emerged from Colombia's social services network as the child most suitable for our family. We were eager to meet Paula. We had been on a nonstop high since getting that referral.

We had so many questions about Paula's homeland – what was it like? Did the people there have enough to eat? Were the houses warm? Did they have McDonalds? And were the people friendly? Would the answers to these questions tell us anything about our new little baby? Maybe not, but I wanted to know everything, even the irrelevant stuff.

Gifts of the Andes

Nestled in the Andean Mountains at 8,500 feet above sea level, Bogotá was unlike any city I'd seen before. Surrounding the airport were thousands of small shacks separated by muddy, unpaved roads. It looked like a good rain could wash the whole community away and I am told that occasionally happened. As we drove from the airport, we could see mostly barefoot people milling about in the evening twilight. Some of the women held babies. I wondered if any of them knew Paula's mother.

Soldiers at the airport stood watch for I don't know what. Military caravans drove through the congested traffic in camouflage-painted trucks at all hours of the day. Soldiers patrolled the hallways of many of the public buildings, like the courthouse where we filed our adoption papers. They carried guns, big guns — guns that looked as if they could blow a hole into the side of a building, let alone the side of a person. At *Unicentro*, a big shopping mall not far from where we stayed, there were machine-gun toting guards at the entryways. Three guards were perched on small stands at the top of streetlamps in the parking area. Even the *Residencias Paris*, where we stayed, featured an armed doorman. Two guards traded shifts so that it was covered 24 hours per day. While I was elated to be in Bogotá to get Paula, I thought it strange that our precious child should come from a place like this. I had never even touched a rifle in my life and here we were about to adopt a baby out of a cradle of guns and guards.

We came to expect animals on our walks through the neighborhood. One house kept roosters and chickens for pets, and we could get close enough to touch them. Sometimes we would find a mule or a horse or a cow tethered to a streetlamp where it was left to graze on the boulevard. I wondered who owned these animals and whether they were ever stolen. Why were they left in the middle of a city?

Most of the buildings more than three stories high were made of red brick. I was told brick was easy to make from the region's natural resources. Bricklayers made pretty good money too. The interior parts of a building – the wiring, plumbing, floors, and walls – must have been a lot harder to come by because we saw many buildings under construction that featured beautiful brick shells that sat empty on the inside. Openings for doors and windows revealed vacant interiors that would need months of work to complete.

The traffic in Bogotá was atrocious, no matter what time it was. We never planned more than two errands per day, even if we were going only a few miles. Driving mostly meant sitting in traffic. Anibal Rojas, the man who drove us around the city, told us that in Bogotá a good horn is as important as a good set of brakes.

The main streets looked like parking lots emptying out after a Vikings game at the old Met Stadium. A sea of vehicles inched along at no more than a few miles per hour, with the aggressive ones seeking an edge by changing lanes. Motorcycles seemed to have the greatest opportunity, their riders largely ignoring the lane markings and driving between cars, even up onto sidewalks. Although the motorcyclists wore reflective vests and displayed their license number on their helmet, they didn't seem particularly safe to me. One wrong move and a car could knock the bike out from under the rider, and who knows whether the car would stop before hitting its owner.

The traffic moved so slowly that vendors walked easily in the streets between cars at intersections. Many, selling gum, candy, magazines, and cigarettes, wore distinctive yellow jumpsuits with logos on their elbows and knees. A local told me the government wants to put these vendors out of business because they pay no sales tax. Children, perhaps no older than 10, also vied for the attention of trapped motorists; they performed acrobatic tricks at the intersections. I saw several children turn perfect cartwheels. Another did a forward handspring. After a few tricks, they raced to the car windows with their hands open.

We heard car alarms sounding all the time. I have no idea whether they were going off accidentally, or whether they truly were deterring would-be thieves. Once, we heard the siren of an ambulance. God pity the victim inside. The ambulance was inching its way through traffic just as we were. I am sure cars would move out of the way, if there was anyplace to move.

Anibal told us that when someone in Colombia needs to get to the hospital in a hurry, they often don't call an ambulance because it takes so long for the vehicle to arrive. Instead, most people rely on friends. Once we saw a man lying on his back in the bed of a pick-up truck, his feet hanging over the end of the tailgate. The pick-up was racing through traffic, weaving between lanes. Anibal said the driver was obviously just trying to get someone to the hospital.

Avenida 19, the nearest busy street, was lined with auto dealerships from companies such as KIA, Mazda, Nissan, and Daewoo. Banks and restaurants were everywhere. Bancolombia, identifiable by its blue, red, brown, and yellow logo, was across the street from Lloyds TSB Bank, where a green-and-white sign promised access to an "easybank" machine. A littler farther down the street was *Banco Ganadero*, a facility that boasted the availability of a Plus Network *Cajero Automatico*, the kind that should operate under the direction of my ATM card. But when I tried it, nothing happened. There was a Taco & Tequila restaurant, next to a *Carbon de Palo*. Other restaurants had names like *Las Lapas* and a *Todo Taco*, in addition to a nice-looking place called *Azzurro Risorante*. A fancy store called the *Galeria Carrion Vivar* featured in its window an oil painting of a freshly cut mango. There was a beauty shop called *Wella*, and a computer store that said it featured technology by Compaq. A bus shelter on the street featured a lush poster advertising something called

"Yanbal." It showed a close-up picture of a pretty girl's face, leading me to believe the product was some kind of makeup. We did most of our shopping for groceries and diapers at a little store called Pomona, where processed foods on the shelves looked exactly like the stuff we were used to buying back home. We particularly grew to like *Postabon*, a Colombian soda pop.

Perhaps the nicest thing about Bogotá was Sunday mornings. Every week, city officials would close off several main thoroughfares for pedestrian traffic. We joined in with crowds of locals, promenading down the center of the otherwise busy street. Vendors took advantage of the situation and set up stands to sell snacks at almost every corner. While we walked, others raced on inline skates or rode their bicycles. On Sundays from early in the morning until 2 p.m., one could enjoy Bogotá in relative peace. The weekly pause in traffic, noise, and pollution was reassuring to me, a visitor, who otherwise found the urban center to be overwhelming, congested, and confusing.

The only place we found in Bogotá to get away from all the hustle and bustle during the week was *Monserrate*, a beautiful lookout at the top of a mountain that towers over Bogotá. From this perch you could see the metropolis that was downtown, a mix of old Spanish architecture and new steel-and-glass structures, like the *Avianca* building that houses Colombia's national airlines. At the top of the mountain, where tourists came, vendors sold a variety of souvenirs not unlike what one would find at Wall Drug or the Wisconsin Dells. Most of the people in Colombia are baptized Catholic, so it was not surprising that at this highest elevation there should be a Catholic church. Susan and I went in. It was a plain sanctuary, cool and dark inside, with smooth, white walls. Near the altar in a horizontal glass case was a statue of Jesus. Depicted fallen under the weight of a wooden cross, Jesus was on the way to Calvary. The image of Christ was painted to show blood and sweat on His face and body. He looked up with big eyes that offer so much hope to many Colombians who found it easier to identify with a fallen Jesus than a triumphant God. The statue had long, lifelike hair and a plaque at the base of the exhibit said the hair was "miraculously" growing.

* * *

March 21, 1995, was Presentation Day, the day we got Paula. We arrived at *Ayudame* mid-morning and were asked to take a seat in the waiting room. Modest vinyl chairs and couches furnished a small room that was lighted by the sun shimmering through a window in the ceiling. The third of four couples to be summoned by the orphanage that day, it was about noon when we were invited into a smartly decorated conference room to discuss the final details. Piedad Sullivan, our LSS representative in Colombia, interpreted instructions from Elsa Márquez Gutierrez, the orphanage director, who told us a little about Paula's history. We signed papers while a nurse went to get Paula.

We waited nervously, and I thought about the random chance of the adoption process. Oh sure, the social worker tries to match a child with a family but in the end it's a crapshoot. As adoptive parents, we'd never really know what we've got until we were living with the child. And at that point, it's undoable – we wouldn't send the kid back. In an effort to mitigate this leap of faith, we had pored over Paula's history and paperwork. We wanted to learn something about her that would prepare us for this moment, ease our nerves, or bring us some peace. But nothing did. The limited amount of information available only led us to speculate and that made our nervousness worse. What if she had an undetected disease? What if she grew up cranky and uncontrollable? What if she hated us?

They brought Paula into the room and put her in my arms. All our fears evaporated. We were no longer nervous, just happy. Paula brought us peace through a huge set of dark eyes that she trained on my face. I think she even smiled. Susan held Paula and she didn't fuss. Paula was plump but oh so light. I held her high in the air and spun around in a circle. The history and paperwork about Paula that we found so frustrating before now meant nothing. We had our little girl and a new Bengtson family was formed. It all seemed so right.

Piedad, a Colombian with a surname from her New Jersey-born husband, and our driver accompanied us out of the orphanage. Euphoric, we floated from meeting to meeting, starting at the courthouse where we filed an adoption petition. A Colombian social services worker conducted an interview in Spanish with the aid of Piedad. Additionally, we had to notarize most of our papers. The *notarias*, the offices housing the notaries, always seemed crowded and we had to wait a long time even to get a couple of papers signed. The final step was to obtain a *sentencia*, the adoption decree that the courts eventually would issue declaring us Paula's legal parents.

Upon completion of the initial meetings, we could spend time getting to know our new baby. In our room at the hostel, we stripped Paula naked and stared at her. We rolled her around on the bed and watched her laugh. Turned out she was a tranquil child, sleeping mostly, and crying only rarely. Susan nursed Paula using a plastic tube and milk bag that hung around her neck. Paula latched onto Susan and the two of them bonded in a way only a mother and child could. I watched in awe, mixing the baby formula for the plastic bags, each of which Paula exhausted in about 15 minutes. Mothering came very naturally to Susan, I could see. I hoped I would be as comfortable as a father.

* * *

A few days after receiving Paula, we were on an errand in Bogotá, congregating around a table at an outdoor café. In the doorway to the restaurant was a large barrel filled with coffee beans. Anibal put his hand in the beans, scooped some up, and popped them into his mouth. He said this was what Colombians did – suck on coffee beans. After a while you would spit them out onto the sidewalk. Well, when in Colombia do as the Colombians do, I thought, so I grabbed a handful. The flavor was uninteresting, exactly what you would expect of coffee beans.

That evening in the middle of dinner, I fell uncharacteristically quiet and excused myself. I never returned. I went up to our room on the second floor and threw up. The walls were thin in the hostel so everyone, I am sure, could hear me. I spent much of the next 12 hours in that bathroom. Then I lay in bed and couldn't move. The hostel had a doctor who examined me and prescribed something, which I drank but I am not sure it did any good.

I couldn't believe this was happening to me. We had been warned about altitude sickness but the thin air didn't affect me; it was the coffee beans, soiled by untold grubby hands. I felt like a slug. Not only did Susan have a new baby to nurse, but now a useless husband. Susan didn't complain. She cared for me like Dad used to take care of our sailboat – with devotion and attention to detail. Susan kept my forehead cool with a damp cloth, and she entertained me by reading aloud from the English-language newspaper we were able to buy. Five days passed and I began to feel human again. The timing was good because the plan was for me to return home that Wednesday, concluding my 10-day stay in Colombia. Susan would remain with Paula until the case was completed.

Sentencia came three weeks later, the Friday before Holy Week when everything in town closed. Back home, the idea of being a father began to sink in. Getting a child was as big as getting married, maybe bigger. When I got married, I became a husband; now I was a husband *and* a father. When I was married, I got a wife; now I have a wife *and* a child. And as demanding as marriage has been, fatherhood would surely be more demanding. As much as I dedicated myself to my wife when I was married, I would now additionally dedicate myself to my child. I had witnessed my dad do so; now it was my turn.

A few days after Easter – the Christian feast of new life – Susan came home with our new baby. Homecoming was a joyous event, with most of Susan's family and me at the airport to welcome Paula and mother.

✳ ✳ ✳

My dad often told a story about the birth of his second child, Peggy, my older sister. Early in the morning, Dad rushed Mom to the hospital. He barely got her in the door when a team of hospital personnel took over. Dad, then a teacher, excused himself to call the high school to let them know he'd need the day off. As he turned around after hanging up the phone, a doctor greeted him with the news that he was now the father of another healthy girl. Dad was stunned, the whole delivery taking less than 10 minutes.

Susan and I had a lot more trouble getting our second child, a boy named John. The next time we went to Bogotá was 20 months later, when we got our referral after another round of paperwork and social services interviews. Dad asked if we planned to wait until after Christmas to get John because a prompt trip would disrupt the traditional family holiday, the referral having come just after Thanksgiving. We thought about it only briefly. If you knew your child was waiting for you in another part of the world, wouldn't you run to him as fast as possible? We couldn't enjoy the holidays in Minneapolis knowing we had a child waiting for us in Colombia. Christmas is about being with family and we now had family in Colombia. We needed to go right away.

But secretly, we expected we might be back by Christmas. We left the first Saturday of December and, adopting for the second time, we thought we might get preferential treatment from the Colombian authorities. We got John the following Monday and the meetings that first week went very smoothly. Even Paula, who came with us, welcomed her new brother with playfulness and the obvious love of a child nearly 2 years old.

Christmas was fast approaching and we watched

with a certain amount of envy as many of the other families at *Las Palmas*, our hostel on this trip, got the okay to leave. December 25 was on a Wednesday and the preceding Thursday was the last day before the courts would close for a three-week break. We knew if we didn't hear that day, we would have to settle in for a long stay. If we got our *sentencia* Thursday, we could complete our paperwork on Friday and Monday, travel on Tuesday, and be home together on Christmas.

Thursday morning, we got word from our adoption representative, Cecilia de Echeverri, that the judge wanted to see us that afternoon. We were elated! This meant *sentencia* and a return by Christmas. We jumped for joy and hugged, we felt so lucky, so fortunate. This would mean only a two-and-a-half-week stay in Colombia, which would be one of the shortest stays ever for such an adoption.

Susan and Cecilia went downtown to the courthouse where Susan expected to sign a few papers and be on her way. I waited at the hostel with Paula and John. Susan, however, had a disastrous afternoon. When she got to the court, the judge refused to issue the *sentencia*. Cecilia pleaded with the judge in every way she could but was unsuccessful. They spent three hours there and the judge wouldn't budge. Susan returned to the hostel in tears.

We could only speculate but we ultimately assumed the judge called all the adoption cases that morning – probably a ritual on the last day before an extended break. When he looked specifically at our case and saw we had only been in the country for two weeks, he probably refused to sign because 10 days isn't very long compared to most adoption cases and he didn't want to set a precedent. Perhaps the judge wanted us to stay longer so we would spend more money in Colombia, which was suffering from recession and everyone knows Americans have money.

* * *

Every other family at *Las Palmas* went home, leaving us alone on Christmas. We were blue but resolved to make the best of it. Susan bought a few gifts for the kids. Christmas morning, we walked down the red-carpeted steps to the main living area on the first floor. A sparsely-decorated, artificial Christmas tree was set up next to the beautiful copper fireplace. Paula was old enough to retrieve gifts from under the tree and open them while John clung to Mom's lap. A maid was on duty and she made breakfast for us. It turned out to be a nice, quiet Christmas morning.

Having been out late the night before, we were tired. Cecilia had invited us to celebrate Christmas Eve with her family, who lived on the north end of Bogotá. Taking up most of the sizeable entryway to their home was a crèche, and at one point we gathered around it, lit candles, and said a prayer. Many of the people in Cecilia's family spoke English and I spent most of my time talking to a brother who sold computers. Cecilia's husband was a college professor; they had a daughter who was studying in Italy. One of Cecilia's brothers came with his wife and their new child. They brought their nanny, who wiped up every spill, changed diapers, and provided comfort in another room when the baby cried. Our own children were in the care of the maid at *Las Palmas*, our ride having arrived after Paula and John had fallen asleep.

Susan and I brought Paula and John to church on Christmas Day. The newer one-story building had a low ceiling that made it difficult to see the altar from the back, where we ended up standing. Eventually, a man offered Susan a seat that she took with John. Paula ended up on the lap of an elderly lady. Most of the people in the filled-to-capacity church were older. The only people in the church younger than we were stood behind us: a little girl with her father and mother, the woman wearing a tight sweater and short skirt. Plastic chairs served as pews on a nicely tiled floor. There were no kneelers but that didn't stop several people from getting down on bended knee at the consecration. I couldn't understand anything the animated priest said but he seemed to hold the attention of the congregation. I couldn't understand the music either, so I don't know whether they actually sang Simon and Garfunkel's "Sounds of Silence" or simply a song with that melody.

The back wall of the church was being painted

and workers had masked an area with newspapers and tape. The newspaper was black and white except for two colorful full-page ads for men's underwear featuring the front and back of a hunky model. They were provocative photos and clearly the person who posted those newspapers hadn't read the catechism's entry on modesty. It was an odd setting, the good-looking bronzed underwear man at the back of the church starring at the crucified body of Christ at the front of the church. Which symbol would the vulnerable souls in the middle choose? Maybe the mother behind me couldn't make up her mind. Maybe many young people had already made their choice and that is why they weren't at Mass.

That afternoon, we left *Las Palmas* to take up our stay at *Residencias Paris*. We needed a change of scenery. I suppose with that Thursday court experience, we associated *Las Palmas* with disappointment. *Paris* was familiar territory. The owner had been friendly to us on the previous trip, and – for whatever reason – a number of other couples were staying there. We hoped the company would help make the time pass quickly.

* * *

Even at *Paris*, however, ennui set in by New Year's Day and we sought a diversion, something Cecilia was able to provide by giving us access to her membership at Anapoyma, a Club Med-like resort not too far from

Bogotá. It seemed like paradise with its huge swimming pool, tennis courts, and golf course but as I prepared to nap under the scalding equatorial sun, I discovered Colombia is full of surprises. A hammock on the patio behind our little cabin was rolled up on the ground. As I unrolled it, a million of the biggest, reddest ants I have ever seen scurried out of the hammock, all over the patio floor. It scared the heck out of me. I rushed back inside the cabin and closed – locked – the sliding door behind me as I looked back at the patio in horror. I overreacted, of course, but it was upsetting. This was a jungle, for crying out loud, and I was confronted with ants the size of rodents. Maybe they were poisonous! They could have attacked Susan or the kids. I was relieved that none of the ants got in the cabin. For the remainder of the day I checked the patio every hour to see what the ants were doing. Mostly they were escaping into the grass, which was fine by me. By the next day, all was quiet but none of us went back out on the patio.

✳ ✳ ✳

The second day after the courts opened following the three-week Christmas break, the judge signed our *sentencia* and we were free to go. The arrangements were set for us to return on a Friday, an early flight necessitating a 4 a.m. wake-up call. Even at that predawn hour, the Avionca terminal at the airport was crowded. We waited in line for our turn with inspectors who went through all of our bags. They thoroughly disrupted our packing and found nothing that bothered them, leaving us to repack while a long line of people waited for us to get out of the way so they could be inspected.

When we got to the ticket counter, they said Paula's visa had expired. Susan and I were dumbfounded. We spoke to a supervisor. She called someone in Miami. As much as we pleaded, they weren't going to let us on the plane. I was tempted to bribe the ticket agent, figuring if they would just let us on the plane I would take my chances with the authorities in Miami. But I didn't try. We had to accept it; we weren't going home that day. I turned around to tell the kids, who could sense something was wrong. Susan sighed; Paula burst into tears. After regaining our composure, we evaluated our options and got our four plane tickets changed to the following Wednesday, hoping we could get everything straightened out by then.

It would have taken us weeks to get Paula another visa but we got a lucky break. Paula's U.S. citizenship came through the day after we left Minnesota to get John. We found out Paula could, in fact, leave Colombia as an American. She just needed the paperwork proving her citizenship. The immigration office that handled the case was in International Falls; we were able to contact that office and ask the authorities there to fax the necessary paperwork to the U.S. embassy in

Bogotá. With that, she could get a transit letter that Avionca would accept.

The American embassy in Bogotá was a new facility protected by police, soldiers and a huge stone wall. A large crowd pressed against a small door that served as the entryway onto embassy grounds. We parked across the street and walked to the front of the crowd. We showed our passports and got right in. Ah, to be an American! Calm greeted us once we got inside the wall.

Several days earlier, Cecilia had invited us to a party hosted by friends, including a couple of Americans who worked in the embassy. The party was being thrown because one of them had just been transferred to the American embassy in Paris. No more hardship pay but a much nicer city to work in than Bogotá. As Susan and I talked to the young State Department employees, it all seemed so glamorous, living in interesting parts of the world, working for Uncle Sam, rubbing elbows with international political figures.

Inside the embassy, waiting to get Paula's paperwork processed, it didn't seem so glamorous. A hundred or more people were waiting for some kind of service and we held a number that seemed impossibly high. Our plane reservations had been rescheduled for the next day. All we could do was sit, wait and hope we would be served before they closed for the day.

Sooner than we expected, however, a woman called our name and we got the papers we needed. We went back to the hostel, packed, ate dinner and pre-pared to leave early the next morning. Departure went smoothly this time. We were at the airport in plenty of time and got to Miami without trouble.

The immigration officer in Miami readily accepted Paula's paperwork. In fact, he even waived a fine that we should have paid for bringing her back without a re-entry visa. Susan, however, was told to go to a room where John's papers would be processed. The room was filled with people from other countries. Susan handed over the paperwork and was told by an indif-ferent attendant to take a seat. Paula and I joined her. We became increasingly frustrated by a lack of activ-ity among the three people "working" in the office. We sat for 45 minutes and absolutely nothing was done. We were on a tight schedule as our connecting flight to Minneapolis was set to leave soon. Susan expressed her concern; an employee responded: "Honey, every-one in this room's got a plane to catch." Susan was fur-ther told to sit and wait.

I was fuming. I got up to leave to make some phone calls to see if I couldn't get these people to hurry up. I'd call the manager of the airport. I'd call the Immigration and Naturalization Service in Washing-ton. I'd call my congressman! Leaving the room, though, turned out to be a mistake. I discovered there was no way for me to get back in. Worse yet, I had the passports, which Susan would need to complete her processing. I explained my desperate situation to a guard and I gave him the passports to return to Susan who was with Paula and John. This actually worked out to our advantage, as far as I can tell. For whatever reason, the office staff, perhaps prompted by the guard's action, suddenly started to process our papers. Once they got going, it only took about 10 minutes. They clearly went out of order, taking our case ahead of all those other waiting people.

In the meantime, I had called home to leave a message on Mom and Dad's answering machine saying we were running into trouble and that I didn't know if we'd catch our scheduled flight.

When Susan got out of that waiting room with the two kids, I was elated. We hugged and exchanged stories, hurrying to retrieve our luggage and get on our flight to Minneapolis. We just barely made it. They literally were closing the gate doors as we arrived. We rushed onto the plane and collapsed into our seats. Paula and John proved remarkably compliant travel companions the rest of the way home.

I was kind of disappointed on the return flight though because I had been unable to call my parents back to tell them we'd be on the originally scheduled flight. The plane we were on didn't have a telephone – the first time I've actually wanted one on an airplane. I was convinced we'd arrive with no one at the gate, which seemed so anti-climactic. We would be getting in around 11:30 at night and we had heard there was a snowstorm in Minneapolis, so I thought there was no way anyone would be there to greet us. But I was surprised. We were the very last ones to get off the airplane and Dave, Susan's dad, poked his head down the jetway to see if anyone else was coming. He saw us, fumbling about with a stroller, two kids, and an assortment of carry-ons. As we came through the jetway and entered the otherwise empty gate area, we were thrilled to find both Susan's parents and my own parents.

Dad said his understanding of my telephone message was that all flight plans were on unless I called with other news. As I hadn't called again, he assumed all along we'd be on the originally scheduled flight. His logic worked. Upon arriving at our home, I saw that Dad had neatly stacked our mail from the previous six weeks on the dining room table. Christmas cards made up the bulk of the stack. We would mail out our own belated Christmas card within a month that included a birth announcement about John. We were glad to be home.

10

Emergence

Soon after Susan and I were married, Dad gave me the sailboat, trailer and all. He knew I was the one who really loved that boat, and Dad found himself less inclined to sail once us kids moved onto lives of our own. Susan and I lived near Lake Harriet, a body of water even better than Nokomis for sailing. A bridge didn't slice the lake in two the way Cedar Avenue did at Lake Nokomis. Plus, there were many more tender boats at Harriet so sailors almost never had to wait to get out to their boat, even at high-traffic times like Saturday mornings. I loved to sail and I loved the *Rose Anne*. I don't really remember the day I received my high school diploma or my college degree, but I remember the day Dad signed the boat deed over to me.

Sailing was a great summer pleasure during those early years of our marriage. I often went with my dad or with friends, but I liked sailing by myself the most. I did my best thinking when I was alone with the wind and the water. Sailing from one end of the lake to the other, I contemplated the significance of life, my efforts that had failed and succeeded, the people I never loved, the fate of the desperate, the good fortune of the undeserving, and the possibilities for a better future. The smell of the air in the middle of the lake was tainted with fish and algae but it filled my lungs with life. I felt strong on the boat; I loved the sensation of sunlight on my chest and back. The main sheet tugged at my hands, irritating the flesh on my palms just a little bit. But I figured it should hurt to harness the wind, gather it into a big white sheet called a sail, and redirect it in such a way that I moved forward through the water. There was no other area of my life where I felt so in control.

One day in August, the water splashed over the bow of the *Rose Anne* as I cut a windward tack on Lake Harriet. I had taken the afternoon off to get away from the pressures of launching *Business Ink*. The spray of the water and the steady breeze compensated for the hot, humid conditions, which surely made the day uncomfortable for the joggers and bikers ringing the lake on the blacktop path. I found the conditions in the middle of the lake to be peaceful, unlike the environment at work, where deadline pressure put tension in the air, and unlike the environment at home, where the activity of two small children made it difficult to relax. When I was a little kid, my parents used to call this late August period the "dog days of summer;" that day, I felt like the luckiest dog around. But I realized it couldn't last.

I had been sailing only one other time that summer. The demands of work and family were cutting into my recreation. I wasn't resentful of the trade-off; I expected to have to grow up at some point and I was coming to understand that I was approaching that point. The day comes for every man when he has to turn in his toys for the responsibility of adulthood, fatherhood, and career endeavors. And it's not as though this concept snuck up on me, I had been thinking about it for years. While we were childless, I had no qualms about leaving the house to sneak off sailing by myself but I had begun to feel guilty about it as the children came into our lives. It wasn't fair to leave Susan with the responsibility of caring for two kids while I was out having fun. Plus, Susan and the kids depended on me. They didn't need me to be off by myself; they needed me to be right there in the house, with them on the floor, playing with the Lincoln logs.

So the boat sat at the buoy, going most of the summer unused. What a sad sight to see a boat wasting away with atrophy. Bird droppings accumulated on the deck and cockpit tarp. Algae grew unfettered on the hull below the waterline. The last two summers, I think I had taken the boat out only a half dozen times. It didn't really make sense for me to keep the boat, I told myself. Plus, I recalled what a hassle it was each fall to borrow a friend's vehicle to tow the boat out of the water and to find storage for it, as our yard wasn't big enough to host a parking place for a boat.

I should sell the boat, I kept telling myself.

I ran a small advertisement in the back of the inaugural edition of *Business Ink*. Being a business publication, I knew it wasn't the best place for the ad, but it was free. And although I would never admit it at the time, I was kind of hoping no one would respond.

I got a call almost the day the publication hit the streets. A woman from one of the western suburbs called to tell me she had learned to sail that summer and was looking for a boat she could keep on Lake Waconia, the same lake I had sailed as a teen with my high school girlfriend and her father. The caller came to our house after dinner as it was getting dark, but apparently she liked what she glimpsed in the twilight because she offered my asking price right there on the spot. As she wrote the check, her husband hitched the trailer to his pickup truck.

"I would be happy to come out after you get the boat launched and show you how the rigging works," I offered.

"Sure. That'd be great," she said without looking at me. "I'll call you."

"Okay. The boat has bailers, you know. They're really useful if you get some water in the cockpit," I said.

"Thanks."

"Oh, do you need me to show you how to step the mast? It's a two-person job," I said. "You have to start from the front of the boat, not the back."

She thanked me again and said she might give me a call, perhaps this fall but more likely next spring. Within minutes, she hopped in the front seat of the pickup and her husband pulled the boat out of my driveway and out of my life.

That next spring, I awaited her call. I thought I could show her the special way I used to hold the tiller with my foot while regulating the sail with my hands. But no call came. When I walked around Lake Harriet, I stopped at the sailing dock, looking for the buoy where the *Rose Anne* had been moored the previous year. A catamaran held the spot now. I noticed that the Park Board had added a tender boat this year. Time passed and the woman who bought my boat still didn't call. By Independence Day, I accepted the fact that she wasn't going to. The *Rose Anne* was gone.

"When the kids get bigger," I thought to myself, "we'll buy another boat."

* * *

I tried to spend as much time with the kids as I could, "family time" becoming very important to me. Susan and I had gone to a lot of trouble to build this little family of ours and I wanted to make the most of it. So I played on the floor with the kids, and tossed them a ball in the back yard, and splashed with them at the wading pool, and took them to the park.

"You have beautiful children," another parent at the park commented as we pushed our kids on the swing set. "What country are they from?"

"Colombia," I answered apprehensively.

"Are they brother and sister?" he asked, motioning to Paula and John.

"They are now," I said.

"No, I mean …"

"I know what you mean," I snapped. "They are brother and sister now, and that is what is important."

I couldn't believe how many people must think it is perfectly okay to walk up to a complete stranger and make some comment about their family. Susan and I were questioned frequently about the kids. Once we were eating in a McDonald's restaurant and an older employee came to our table.

"The children are beautiful," she said looking at Susan and me. "Are they yours?"

"Certainly they are," I said.

"I mean, are they adopted?" she persisted.

"They are from Colombia," Susan said.

"Are they brother and sister?"

"Absolutely!"

"That's so nice." She finally went away.

I wondered if she came up to other families and asked about the relationship among the siblings. Did she tell other parents that it was nice that their children have siblings? The well-meaning lady and the other parent at the park really upset me. Why were they inquiring about my family? Was adoption so strange? Does it matter where the kids came from? Wasn't it enough that we were a family and that Mom and Dad were making every effort to raise them well? They thought that just because the kids have darker skin than either Susan or I, that they had the right to ask me personal questions about my family. Once a guy looked at Paula and told me, "She must have a very beautiful mother." I didn't know what to make of that comment. "She does," I answered.

Sometimes the questioner wouldn't take a hint and kept asking questions despite my obvious discomfort.

"Do you know anything about the parents?" they would ask, or "What do you know about their medical history?"

One woman asked, "Oh, who could give up such a beautiful child?"

Someone else commented: "What's wrong with Colombia that they have so many children to give away?"

The thing that irked me so much about these kinds of comments was the lack of consideration for our children. They said them right in front of Paula and John, as if the kids couldn't understand. But they could, even if they were young. Once Susan asked Paula how she felt when a stranger came up to us and started asking questions about her adoption.

"It makes me feel like I'm not really part of the family," Paula said.

Okay, that was it. We had to come up with a way to respond to the comments. "None of your business," worked fine for me, but Susan said that was too rude. Susan discussed the situation with other adoptive parents, none of whom had any particularly satisfying responses.

Susan and I came up with two strategies. If the stranger asked a question about one of the kids, Susan or I would turn to the child and ask if they wanted to answer the question. If they said no (which is what they always said), then we responded that the child didn't want to talk about it. Most people were unwilling to press something at the risk of upsetting a child. The other strategy was to ask the questioner "Why do you want to know that?" This would help them to see the shallowness of their question and they would back away. Or, if they persisted without giving a good reason, then Susan or I felt a little better about declining to answer. It was possible, however, that the stranger had a good reason for the question. If, for example, they told us they were considering adoption themselves and wanted to know what it has been like for us, then we were inclined to take their questions more seriously.

✳ ✳ ✳

Within a year after the *Business Ink* debacle, I hired three strong-willed employees to replace those who had left. Although Jackie and I were the ones with the experience, the new hires all had their own ideas. I tried to give everyone the freedom to direct their own work but clashes started to erupt as we proceeded with one of our most important projects since I bought the company – a complete redesign of *Northwestern Financial Review*. The magazine was the backbone of the company, generating enough revenue to give us the freedom to experiment with things like *Business Ink*. I felt the magazine needed to keep up with the times, so in early 2000 we conducted a readership survey; then we surveyed our advertisers. With the survey results, we came up with a strategy for reformatting *Northwestern Financial Review* with a new look. More important, we increased the magazine's distribution and created opportunities for advertisers. We would work on the redesign all fall and unveil the updated magazine with the first issue of 2001.

I had always told the employees that I valued their opinions, and the new ones had a lot of opinions about what the redesigned magazine should look like. They offered me their thoughts and expected me to implement them. I considered their suggestions but they rarely squared with my vision so I didn't follow up on them. Jackie and I had put a lot of work into the redesign effort over a period of about a year; we were much more concerned about pleasing our readers and advertisers than we were about pleasing our staff. Although I felt on track about my efforts to please the marketplace, I knew I was missing the boat in my own shop. Half the staff was growing discontented and it worried me.

Ever since I got into business I had heard about other companies that conducted retreats, off-site events, or team-building sessions. I had just been to a convention where a speaker discussed the team-building exercises she conducted for a client. I gave her a call. She agreed to come in for a half a day and work with my staff. She would ferret out the challenges we faced in working together and give us suggestions for building a more effective team.

I told the staff about it and the response was favorable. We agreed to make it an all-day, off-site event. The consultant would occupy our morning and we would spend the afternoon on some other helpful exercise. We decided that everyone would make a half-hour presentation on the subject of their choice. I figured we could all get to know each other a little better that way, and it would give everyone the opportunity to build their communication and presentation skills.

That first Thursday in November, we all met at the Arboretum, a trendy host for these kinds of corporate events. Although we were only a group of six, the consultant relied on an overhead projector and microphone to explain to us the characteristics of a successful company. She gave each of us a bright yellow rubber band to wear on our wrist. Each had a saying on it, such as "There is no I in Team" and "Winners never quit." She told us that too often people fall into negative patterns of communication. "If you ever catch yourself saying something negative, pull on your wristband and let it snap back against your skin," she said. The pain was supposed to deter us from future forays into negativity. "And if you catch someone else saying something negative, go up to them and gently tug at their wristband," she said. "They'll get the idea."

The morning centered on a test the consultant administered. The results would indicate personality types. Each of us was asked to answer a series of 100 wide-ranging questions, some of which seemed to have little to do with work. We were asked if we liked to work individually or in groups. If we preferred long lunches or a good coffee break. If we liked to read a good book or go to the movies. A computerized answer sheet accompanied each test. As we blackened the appropriate response for each question with our No. 2 pencil, the consultant played New Age music on her boom box. It was kind of like taking the SATs, only not as stressful. No answers were considered wrong.

The consultant analyzed the results immediately, plotting them on a chart that she displayed with the overhead projector. A couple of people were deemed "strong creative," another was labeled "analytical," and I was called "demanding." We spent the last hour of the morning talking about these characteristics. We discussed strategies for people with seemingly incompatible styles to work together. Communication was a major stumbling block at most companies, we were told, so we talked about the varying ways people like to communicate. Some of my colleagues liked face-to-face communication, another preferred to communicate through memos, and still another preferred e-mail. The consultant said that if we knew how others wanted to be communicated with, we should accommodate those wishes if we all wanted to get along well.

The consultant said that getting along was mostly a matter of making concessions, a conclusion I found unsatisfying. Why is it that someone with 20 years of work experience should compromise with someone only a few months out of school? It seemed unfair, if not ridiculous, to me. I believed getting along was more about knowing your role in an organization and respecting the expertise of those around you. Boundaries need to be honored. Someone needs to be in charge; consensus management in a small company is nonsense.

Call me stubborn, but the consultant failed to tell me anything that changed my mind. Granted, I may have needed to do a better job communicating what was expected of everyone. And, if nothing else, I now knew that I should put my thoughts in a memo for one employee, email them to another, and have a face-to-face meeting with the rest.

The consultant concluded her portion of the day by distributing little orange placards containing 12 "Tips for Understanding Other People." Suggestions included "Accept differences in others," "Be patient with and tolerant of others," and "Choose positive, not negative or neutral, attitudes."

About a week after the retreat, I received a report generated by the consultant. It described the highlights of the day, with additional analysis of the test results. She said that everyone in the company should be able to work together well, except Jackie. The consultant said she was too strong-headed to work well with others, and that I should reconsider her role with the company if staff harmony was my goal.

The report confirmed what I had suspected since about 10 o'clock on the morning of the off-site: the consultant had everything backwards. Jackie was the best employee I ever had. She was the only one who had any appreciation for the nature of a small business. She was the only one who had enough experience to know what NFR Communications was all about. And she was the only one who labored more for the sake of doing good work than for her paycheck.

Ultimately, the consultant's report did get me thinking about Jackie's role with the company – it needed to be bigger. I had taken NFR Communications as far as I could on my own. During the 1990s, we had tried a few things with varying degrees of success, but I had a lot more things I wanted to try. For example, I had this idea about a consumer magazine distributed through community banks. We'd be the perfect company to create such a publication but I was already maxed out. My plate was full. I needed a partner. I couldn't do it all on my own.

But, oh, what a wrenching thought. I had been through a partnership before and it was difficult. Bob Cronin was my good friend but we clashed on key business points. We were lucky to maintain a friendship after dissolving the partnership. Would I be so lucky if I tried it again? Who could I trust? I think I could trust Jackie. She saw potential in the company, she was willing to invest her energy into it. I could see that, even if the consultant couldn't. But I remembered my dad's experience. I remembered him telling me he chose to limit his business to a size he could manage on his own. Dad was a very smart guy and if he chose not to find a partner and grow, there had to be a good reason. Dad built a successful company on his own and retired in comfort. Would I be sorry if I took another route?

Dad's example had always meant so much to me; it had been my reliable guide. Like Dad, I earned my own way, made my own decisions, and made pretty good money along the way. Why would I change? Maybe I couldn't help it, like a boy can't really help but eventually grow into a man. A boy with a good father is lucky to have an example in his youth, but perhaps when he grows up he needs to look inside himself for direction more than to others. It could have been my growing family, or it could have been the encouragement of a loving wife, or it could have been the loyalty of a good employee — I'm not sure — but

I realized that I wanted to do more and I knew I needed help.

I finally understood: I am not my father. I could trust a partner. The next day I offered Jackie the position of president of NFR Communications, and she accepted.

The staff was surprised by the news; they didn't necessarily approve and within a few months three employees left the company. We rebuilt the staff, Jackie doing a better job hiring than I had done. And we turned our attention to other projects. Jackie developed a business plan for that consumer magazine and we launched it in summer 2002.

I felt a great freedom after deciding to share the company leadership with a trusted friend, a friendship forged by the ups and downs of the business during the previous five years. I knew there weren't any guarantees about the success of this partnership. Perhaps it would end no more successfully than my partnership with Cronin. Perhaps growth would remain elusive and I would never do much more than publish a banking magazine with a very small readership. Perhaps my company would never grow any larger than Dad's company. I couldn't know for sure unless I tried.

I had to try.

11

Fatherhood

The addition of our third child, Catherine, changed the dynamic of our household back to what I had known as a kid. The childs' play was louder than it had been with a smaller family; toys were strewn about and it seemed someone was always running around. Catherine brought us so much life and helped me see deeper into the meaning of parenting. Susan and I knew all along we wanted a family made up of more kids than parents. We wanted a family that grew according to trust, which we happily exchanged for the control we exercised under the one-child-per-parent arrangement.

Catherine's adoption, which took place on April 12, 1999, was the smoothest of the three. The biggest difference this time was the size of our entourage to Bogotá, as we brought Paula and John with us. The highlight of the trip, next to receiving Catherine, was a week's vacation in Cartagena. We had stayed pretty close to Bogotá on our previous trips while more adventurous adoptive couples traveled about, returning with stories about the magnificent Colombian landscape.

The U.S. State Department, however, warned against travel into the Colombian countryside, where a civil war had raged for 40 years. I read once in the *New York Times* that 3,500 people per year die in the fighting. Thousands are kidnapped, some never to be seen again. The fighting, which started in the 1960s, involved three groups of people: the rebels, the paramilitary, and the Colombian government. With only a small middle class, Colombian society consisted of a wealthy, controlling class and a huge class of underprivileged. A group among the poor — farmers mostly — began to wage war against the government, believing no changes were in store through the normal democratic process. These rebels destroyed plantations and other property belonging to the wealthy. Unable to rely on the Colombian police or army for protection, the wealthy hired paramilitary forces to fight back. The drawn-out fighting sapped much of the idealism that originally motivated the rebels. The largest rebel group was called FARC, a Spanish acronym for the Revolutionary Armed Forces of Colombia. I was told the rebels funded their efforts through the sale of drugs, Colombia being the largest supplier of cocaine to the United States. Bolivia and Peru used to grow a lot of coca, the plant from which cocaine is made, but the United States and others funded programs in those countries to eradicate the crop. Most of the coca growers simply moved to Colombia.

In addition, the rebels funded their efforts through extortion. Locals explained it to me like this: In small towns, they would go to business owners and say "pay me every month or we will burn your business down." The shop-owners had no choice but to pay or to close down and move, which was what many people did. Bogotá, ill-equipped to handle the onslaught, brimmed with the transplants, many of whom found they couldn't re-open their business. Scores ended up begging in the streets.

The rebels were also famous for kidnapping wealthy people and demanding ransom. A few days after we arrived in Colombia to get Catherine, a small Avionca airplane was hijacked by rebels. Flying from Bucaramanga to Bogotá, the airplane was forced to land on a jungle airstrip where about 40 people were taken hostage. By the time I left two weeks later, no one had heard from any of those kidnap victims. Almost a year after the incident, a Colombian nun told us the hostages were still missing. We knew a couple adopting a baby who was supposed to be on that flight. It left on a Monday morning but this couple, having already picked up their baby in Bucaramanga, changed their tickets to take the Sunday night flight back to Bogotá. You should have seen their jaws drop when they read in the newspaper what had happened.

Emerging Son

The only place the U. S. State Department said was safe was Cartagena, so that's where we went. We traveled on AeroRepublica, the cheap-o domestic airline, landing at Cartagena's quaint airport. The airplane back-taxied on the landing strip to the terminal since there was no taxi lane. Small, general aviation aircraft like the kind I learned to fly do this all the time at the smallest airports but I never imagined that a commercial jet might back-taxi. We taxied faster than I could ever remember a jet moving on the ground, and when we reached the tarmac in front of the terminal building I realized why. Another airplane landed moments after we cleared the runway. These two planes were playing chicken.

Cartagena is a beautiful, old, walled city on the ocean. We walked the narrow streets inside the wall, where it was hot, humid, and crowded. Our villa had two small pools, and the water was warm and clear. The villa, which we had secured with the aid of Cecilia, who remained our LSS representative, was spacious with accommodations for perhaps three or four families. We stayed on the second floor where a balcony surrounded most of our living space, which consisted of a kitchen/living area and two bedrooms, each with its own bathroom. The ceilings were 15 feet high and the walls were three feet thick, which we could see at the windows. The doors were glass from floor to ceiling. A porter, who was on the grounds nearly all the time, helped us with our bags, cleaned the pools, brought us phone messages, and served as our doorman. A cook made breakfast and lunch for us. A large, dark-skinned woman, the cook was gentle with our children and I have a vivid image of her holding Catherine against her chest as she comforted her in a rocking chair on the third floor where we took most of our meals.

The space was beautiful but unforgiving for a child. Tile everywhere, all the surfaces were hard, as in "hurt-your-head-when-falling-down." The stairs were steep, and the balcony always made me nervous but these were minor details in an otherwise magnificent place. Cartagena's clean, moist air was more appealing than the dusty air we breathed at high altitudes in Bogotá. This sea-level air was thick and fresh. The streets were busy but it was all together different from Bogotá. The clip-clop of horse hooves provided a beat for the street noise here. Performers in the squares came out as the sun went down. The palm trees and beach reminded us we were in the Caribbean.

But we also saw the young boys who got through life by sniffing glue, and we saw the street vendors who sold it. The museums were filled with information about the evils of centuries ago – the Inquisition, the slave trade. We also learned about heroes, like St. Peter Claver who lived in Cartagena and helped so many of the slaves. Today a large church in Cartagena is named after him. The tranquility of the Sabbath particularly impressed me. Every other day of the week the streets were bustling with activity but on the Sunday we were there the stores stayed closed and no one was on the streets.

Within a few days of returning to Bogotá after the weeklong sojourn, I went home with Paula and John. Susan stayed in Colombia with Catherine until her adoption case worked its way through the courts – which was about another three weeks. Susan would return the end of May, so I had a month ahead of me as a single parent. With the essential aid of friends and relatives, the time went quickly. By now, *Residencias Paris* had e-mail so I sent Susan a message every day. I wrote her love notes like I've never written before and I'm sure she thought I was crazy but I wasn't. I was in love with my wife and it only became more obvious to me during this period of separation.

The last day of May, Susan was set to return home; she would be coming through Houston, exactly as I had done with Paula and John a month earlier. So I went down to Houston to meet her and accompany her back to Minneapolis. Susan was to get in around mid-day and have a lengthy layover until her flight for Minneapolis left at eight that evening. I left Paula and John with friends the night before and took a morning flight to Houston. I knew where the foreign arrivals would be exiting and I waited for almost two hours before she emerged, pushing a small stroller with Catherine in it. She looked great and I was so happy to see her. We hugged and hugged and kissed.

The Houston airport has a Marriott Hotel attached

to it and I had arranged a room there for the day. I walked her to the hotel where we spent the entire lay-over. Catherine was sound asleep in the stroller when Susan and I embraced on the bed. I don't know if it was an expression of pent-up passion, just a release of tension, or true love, but Susan and I made love and it never felt so good. When the air cleared we lay side by side, sharing our thoughts about the previous month and about our future. I felt like I did when we had just married – giddy, romantic, hopeful, optimistic. We closed out our eight-hour stay with a room-service din-ner before boarding the plane and heading back home. The next morning, we picked up the other two kids and settled into our life in southwest Minneapolis as a family of five.

* * *

Sometimes I wondered if I was a good father. I found it so easy to lose my patience and say something I didn't mean, or do something I regretted, like holler or kick something in frustration. Was I a decent hus-band? Susan wanted a good father for the children so if I failed as a father I was also failing as a husband. The stakes were so much higher than they were when we were first married.

My dad's example taught me one way to be a good father: take the family on trips. One of the first summers after getting Catherine, Susan and I took the kids to the Black Hills, a 600-mile drive over South Dakota prairie from the Twin Cities. We were, by then, the owners of a mini-van and we gave it a real work-out in the 100-degree heat of that August vacation. It took two days to get there, and another two days to return, so the majority of our week-long vacation took place inside that Pontiac Montana.

"Dad, what's Wall Drug?" Paula asked, as we drove west along Interstate Highway 90.

"A tourist trap near the Black Hills," I said.

"What's a tourist trap?" John asked.

"A place where you can buy junky trinkets that are supposed to remind you of your trip."

"Can we buy something, please, please, please?" Paula asked.

"We're not stopping at Wall Drug," I said. "If we want to buy junk, we can go to the discount store at home anytime we want."

"Dad, are we almost there yet?" John asked. We were just pulling into Mitchell, where we planned to see the famed Corn Palace.

"No, we're a long ways away," I answered.

"Are we staying in a hotel with a pool?" Paula asked as she stared out onto the parched landscape.

"I'm not sure," I answered, knowing perfectly well there was no pool at our destination but I didn't want to get into a fight over it.

"I sure hope so," Paula said. "It's hot."

Susan saw my strategy and tried to take Paula's

mind off of the heat. "Let's play the alphabet game," Susan suggested.

"Okay, I see an A," said John, pointing to a Wall Drug sign.

The travel time on a family vacation is as important as the time at the destination, and little games made the time go faster. Susan was the master of the road trip, preparing snacks, music, games, and picture books.

We found the Black Hills to be magnificent. It seemed so much more interesting to me now than it did when Mom and Dad brought the family here 30 years earlier. Mount Rushmore was spectacular, particularly during the night lighting ceremony. Paula seemed to have an interest in history and asked why those four presidents were selected. John liked the uniform that the National Parks ranger was wearing. Catherine was too small to notice much but clearly she was content in her stroller absorbing the sun and friendly smiles from other tourists.

Family travel was nice but a vacation was an exception. Most of the interaction Susan and I had with the kids was mundane. For example, we liked to take the kids on walks around the block. Paula and John had bicycles with training wheels and Catherine had a plastic tricycle with pedals, although usually she propelled herself without them. A walk around the block was a little like what I imagined the Lewis and Clark expedition was – slow and full of discovery. Paula and

John started out energetically on their bikes. They raced ahead, and Susan and I had to remind them to stop at every driveway to look for cars. Catherine charged out like she wanted to keep up with the older two but she was soon distracted by a bit of sand on the sidewalk. She got off her tricycle and picked up a handful of sand, letting the small particles fall through her fingers. She repeated her action a dozen times. Susan stayed with her while I tried to keep up with Paula and John. Susan encouraged Catherine to recommence her forward progress. She was successful only for a few feet before Catherine found a dandelion to examine. John and Paula, meanwhile, had found a puddle on the sidewalk near the bakery on the corner. They set aside their transportation and stepped into the curbside pool. "Stay out of the water!" I shouted in a command they obliged only after too much lingering.

Outside the bakery, a customer had tied a dog to a signpost. The kids were immediately attracted to its panting mouth, furry exterior, and wagging tail. "Wait, wait, you can't just pet someone else's dog. You don't know if that dog is friendly," Susan said. The owner came out. "Is it okay if my kids pet your dog?" I asked. "Sure," and the kids descended upon the poor beast. They stroked the dog with both their hands. Out of the 30 fingers messaging this animal, only four remained visible in the thick, long fur. "Dad's allergic to dogs," Paula informed her siblings. "We will never get a dog so we have to pet other peoples' dogs."

As the walk continued, Susan and I were never sure if the kids would successfully negotiate the 90-degree turn at each corner. Sometimes they forgot to turn and ended up going straight into the street. Last summer, John attempted the same turn three times and fell over after each effort – a significant feat with training wheels. After several minutes of comforting, the wailing subsided. This time however, with a solid verbal reminder, everyone made the turn.

The block was not entirely level. While the kids greatly enjoyed the slight down-hill slope at the beginning of the walk, they complained in the face of the slight ascending incline on the back of the block. Complaining came a little too easy to Paula and John, Susan and I believed. Faced with even the slightest adversity, the kids surrendered. We encouraged them to keep peddling but they got off their bikes and walked the rest of the way. Catherine was the only one loyal to her wheels. Paula and John ran off. "Hey, don't leave your bikes!" I shouted. "Daddy, can you get them?" Paula yelled. "No," I said. "If you don't come get them we'll just have to leave them and they will probably be stolen!" Paula and John came back for their bikes, grabbing a single handlebar to tow them behind as they walked.

The last 100 yards of the walk were on level ground. The kids remounted their wheels and sped home. Susan and I enjoyed the walk. Originally we thought these kinds of walks might offer some value along the lines of exercise but the slow pace rendered that potential benefit moot. For Susan and me, the real benefit was the time together, which we got far too little of. The fresh air was nice, especially in Minnesota where we spend way too much time indoors waiting out the cold of our lengthy winters. Parenting is much more difficult from November to April because the kids are confined to the indoors. Oh sure, you can go out during those months but only after spending 45 minutes dressing the kids in thick socks, long underwear, snow pants, coats, hats, scarves, mittens, and boots. Even with all the warm clothing, our kids never seemed to want to stay out in the cold for more than a half-hour or so. Most of the winter days were spent inside where the confines of our home seemed to induce petty arguing and fighting among the kids. They played nicely together about 90 percent of the time but we usually forgot about that dealing with the 10 percent of the time when they were fighting. Sometimes the only escape was the television set, an option that carried a certain amount of guilt for parents who really wanted something better for their kids than what was offered by the typical television network or Disney video.

I was finding fatherhood magnificent. I loved reading stories to the children on the couch. Sometimes we played "school" in the basement and I got to teach them real things like the name of the Mississippi River, the location of the Great Lakes, or the United States' proximity to South America. They thought my lesson was a game; little did they realize they were really learning. I loved teaching them to throw a ball, something all three kids could do with varying degrees of proficiency. Some of the teaching was tedious, like getting them to sit up at the dinner table and use silverware. Or getting them to use a tissue when they had a runny nose. Or getting them to pick up their toys. Or make their bed. Or hang up their jacket. But most of our time together was rewarding. I could already see that they grow up fast.

※ ※ ※

Susan and I wrestled with the question of whether to adopt again. We were always open to a pregnancy but we didn't really expect that to happen. Although we would welcome another adopted child, I dreaded the process — the endless meetings, paperwork, and red tape that go along with any process involving the government and the social services world. From an efficiency perspective, government and social services are a combination from hell, and with adoption I threw myself at their mercy. Plus, as we considered another adoption, there was Colombia itself to think about. The country was getting more violent all the time. Did we want to put ourselves at risk of kidnapping or worse? And what about the three kids we have? Should we bring them along? What kinds of risks would we be exposing them to? How do you weigh the potential danger against the importance of the entire family be-ing together on presentation day? We contemplated all these questions.

Sometimes I thought about what would happen if we were to lose a child. What if Paula or Catherine became ill and died? What if John ran out into the street and was killed by a car? Would their lives and all of our efforts up until then have been wasted? Would it all have been for nothing? I think of what life might have been like for John if he had stayed in the *barrios* of Bogotá. For the promise of food every day, perhaps he would have been recruited into one of the revolution-ary armies, only to be separated from the rest of his family and probably killed at a young age. How tragic it would be if the United States were to get itself into a war, reinstate the draft and John found himself fight-ing just the same. Had I really improved his life any?

You almost have to have a large family if you ex-pect to raise even one child to a dignified adulthood. But then, Mom and Dad had five kids and we all grew up okay. I couldn't help but wonder to what extent our family size related to our well-adjusted upbring-ing. When I become old, I wondered, would I look back and ask: "Why didn't we adopt that fourth child?" Would I exclaim: "We should have done it! What were we afraid of?"

Why do we have children anyway? It's a ques-tion that seems particularly relevant to adoptive par-ents. Unlike biological parents, we can't claim any child was unexpected. We took very deliberate, complicated steps to assure our place as parents. Why?

I was responding to a deep inner yearning – a yearning that almost seems in conflict with itself as I was seeking to reclaim my childhood and at the same time seeking my adulthood. I wanted that family I grew up with. Childhood was such a positive, loving, and happy time for me, I wanted it again. But I also wanted to grow up. Like any living creature, I wanted to become what I am – that is, an adult. And somehow I grew to believe that a typical man approaching 40 should know the love of a wife and kids, the security of home, and meaningful work. As a kid watching my dad, I never realized what a big deal it was to have all this; now I know.

The same way a baby emerges from the familiar comfort of the womb into the unknown, harsh but opportunity-filled world, a man exchanges a carefree, self-centered existence for the uncertain but potentially joyous responsibility of fatherhood. I am grateful for the time I had as a single man, and for the time I had with Susan before we had children, but I am so grateful for this period. Parenthood demands love and trust and faith like no other period in life I have known. Fatherhood is helping me to replace my natural-born selfishness with selflessness. Maturity is figuring out that the whole world doesn't revolve around me, and fatherhood is helping me to see that, and more important, to embrace that. I found my home in fatherhood. Now my job, which could take decades, is to help my kids find their home.

I want the same thing for my children as I want for myself: I want them to work all their lives to replace their natural human selfishness with earnest selflessness. Love that can change the world comes from a selfless heart. Susan and I will give our kids opportunity. They will go to good schools. We will show them many wonderful places in the United States and the world. And I will support them, no matter what their vocation. Their pursuit of any demanding, honest work will make me proud. But people don't change the world by what they do, they change the world by who they are. And I pray my children grow to become the selfless heroes that the world so desperately needs.

* * *

When the Boat Show came to the Twin Cities again, I thought maybe I'd go; perhaps I'd take along John or Paula. When I told them about it, they both said they wanted to come with me. At the show, they seemed more interested in the soda pop and popcorn than sailboats and racing gear. But they tagged along, watching me examine the masts and sails. They followed as I climbed in and out of each cockpit. I ran my hand along the deck on boats with wood finishes. They thought I was just looking at boats but I was connecting my past with my future.

That night, the kids wanted me to tell them a bed-time story. Even Catherine, who was too young to sit still long enough to listen to one, wanted a story. And they wanted me to make up a story, not simply read one out of a book. I wasn't very good at making up stories. "Kids, I can't think of any stories," I said. But they pleaded, their big eyes and wide smiles thrust into my face. This happened many evenings. I would do the best I could, inevitably drawing on some real-life boyhood experience.

"Mark and Todd had just finished playing tennis and were going to Mark's house. They walked through the alleyway, past the garbage cans that everyone kept out back by their garage. As the two boys walked, they spied a treasure trove. Someone was throwing away a collection of hunting magazines! The boys stopped and looked. The glossy magazines featured pictures of wild game. The boys wanted to bring the magazines home but they would have to come up with a way to get them past Mark's mom, who would be sitting in the kitchen. Remembering an old cardboard box in the garage, they devised a plan ..."

12

Epilogue

We resolved that nagging question about a fourth child by adopting Michael. We got his referral on November 7, 2002; leaving for Bogotá on November 18, the plan was for Paula and me to return to Minneapolis on November 26, leaving Susan, and the rest of the kids to remain through the conclusion of the case.

Bogotá seemed a little cleaner than it did three years earlier. *Aveneda 19*, the main thoroughfare two blocks from our hostel, had been newly paved and a bike path had been constructed in the median. Sidewalks along the busy roads had been reconstructed in brick, and there were benches and waste receptacles lining the walkways that weren't there in 1999. The traffic, however, looked as congested as ever.

We stayed at a hostel called Zuetana, a word meaning "home" in a South American Indian language. The hostel had 10 rooms and while we were there it was completely full with eight other couples, one less than capacity because we were using two rooms. Two couples came from Norway and one came from Denmark. Two couples were from France and one was from Australia. Most of the couples were adopting their first child. I think some of them didn't know what to make of us. One of the women from France asked why we wanted four children. A man asked me if I was sure we knew what we were doing.

Things also looked better at *Ayudame*, where they had installed an elevator since we had been there in 1999. A sheriff and his wife were adopting a 2-year-old at the same time we were, so we talked as we waited to be invited to the conference room where we would be briefed on our children. Cecilia, once again our representative from Lutheran Social Services, introduced us to Maria Clemencia Marquez Gutierrez, who was now the director of the orphanage. The nine of us (six adults and our three children) found our places in the conference room, the children playing with toys while the sheriff and I nervously ate chips and nuts offered as snacks.

With Cecilia translating, Maria Clemencia provided a medical history for each of the children. No surprises, so we signed – three forms in triplicate – and prepared to greet our new babies. The other couple moved to another room where they got their child first. Then came Michael. Maria Clemencia brought him to us in her arms, making a dramatic entrance down a staircase, which we captured on videotape. Michael was beautiful. He was all smiles as we passed him between the various members of the Bengtson family, pausing only for photos. He never cried. He beamed until he fell asleep in the car on our return to the hostel. A chaotic scene broke out at Zuetana upon our arrival, with the hostel staff and other couples vying for a peek at the new baby.

When we finally got Michael into his crib, Susan and I stared at him. He was big for his age, with features lighter than the other three children. His hair, brown, perhaps even reddish. His skin was as pale as mine. Cecilia said the baby looked like me. Strange. I wondered if the orphanage staff matched Michael to our family because we looked alike.

Paula, John, and Catherine smothered Michael with affection. Paula was a little mother, bringing him bottles and checking his diaper. John walked around with his chest puffed out, proud to have a little brother, or perhaps more likely, proud to be a big brother. And Catherine understood that she had one more playmate. But adding a child to the family was a big change and we definitely were in a transition period. Catherine didn't necessarily like the idea that she wouldn't get all the attention that came with being the youngest in the family. Paula was really hoping for a little sister. And even Dad had to admit that he was a little jealous that Susan would have one more person to pay attention to, leaving a little less attention for him. A bigger family meant we'd all have to work a little harder to keep harmony in our home.

A nun we visited on the day before Paula and I left for home helped me understand the importance of a peaceful home. Her name was Sister Margaret. Months earlier, Susan had become acquainted with an order of nuns living in Rochester, Minnesota, that runs a mission in Bogotá. They invited Susan to contact the mission on our next trip to Colombia. Susan put the call in and the very next day a van appeared at our front door, ready to take us to the *barrio* where the sisters ran schools and a convent.

The van driver took us up the side of one of the mountains located north of Bogotá. Thousands of squatters had built a city out of uneven bricks, miscellaneous pieces of lumber, and corrugated sheets of metal. The locals called it the "invasion," referring to the people who had fled the countryside seeking refuge in Bogotá, where the armed guerrillas couldn't threaten them. But without money and with few marketable skills, they took up any free residence they could. This meant living in a hovel they either built themselves or found after some other family had moved out. These neighborhoods cropped up during the last 40 years at all borders of the city. They existed extensively on the city's south side, near the airport, and in this northeast corner where our van driver was about to drop us off in front of a school. Many of the *barrios* lack running water and electricity although the area we were touring did have these amenities, plus rare paved roads, albeit at such steep grades that they must have been useless for older vehicles.

"Welcome," said Margaret, who said she didn't like to use the title "sister" with her name. We shook hands and introduced ourselves. Margaret was small, no more than 90 pounds, but she was surefooted on the uneven path and spoke with urgency. She wore glasses that were fashionable about a decade ago, a small wooden cross on a string necklace, and a blue-green windbreaker that distinguished her from the locals. Her skin was browned by years of exposure to Central American climate. She explained she had worked in the poorest parts of El Salvador and Peru before coming to Bogotá in 2001.

The school, she explained pointing to a turret over the entryway, was once a castle. She showed us around, initially passing a room where children received dental care from a volunteer dentist. Before the school came along, tooth decay, gum disease and other oral plagues afflicted most of the children. Margaret showed us other rooms where adults were leading groups of children in creative activities. The rooms were bright and decorated with papier-mâché artifacts and cutouts made of construction paper. A circular stairway in the turret led to a meditation room where Margaret said the sisters prayed.

The castle was one of four schools the sisters operated. This one was for young children, but there was also a school for pre-teens and another for teenagers. The one for older kids offered education in trades such as baking and carpentry. Plus they had recently started a school for "the people who are not in school." People of any age could drop in whenever they liked to learn basics such as reading and math. Margaret led us down a steep road to the school for pre-teens. On the way, we walked past a number of wild dogs, their lethargic pace and protruding ribs indicating severe malnourishment. Margaret told Paula, John, and Catherine not to go near the dogs, a needed warning since the kids would never make a distinction between the well-treated pets back home and these neglected beasts.

Arriving at the school for older kids, we encountered groups of students in the schoolyard doing exercises. They were sitting on the bumpy ground in their uniforms stretching for their toes. "One of the biggest problems we encounter in the *barrio*," explained Margaret, "is that the kids have under-developed motor skills and muscles because they sit around all day in their houses." She said many of the kids come to school unable to hold a pencil. Some limped or had other mobility problems. So at school they received a certain level of physical therapy designed to strengthen their muscles. "I visit many of the families and when they invite me in, there often is no chair to sit on. We sit on the floor or on a bed," she said. "They have nothing to do, so they lie around much of the day and that leads to some of the problems we try to deal with here."

She explained that few of the people in the *barrio* work for wages. The men, she said, sometimes got jobs in construction, a trade that was entirely dependent upon the fortunes of the economy. Things were slow in Colombia at the moment, so not many of the men were working. The women, she said, got jobs in Bogotá doing housekeeping. I had noticed with some envy the fact that even middle class families often had maids in Colombia. I was once told a maid is not very expensive in Bogotá. I wondered now whether such employment was exploitative or helpful.

"Do you have any way of tracking what happens to the students once they complete the schooling offered here?" I asked.

"No," said one of the English-speaking counselors at the school. "Most do not go on to college, although two or three per year will get a scholarship. Some of the others will get jobs. We have a program to get some of them internships with companies such as American Airlines. But most of them, we will never hear from again and I have no idea what will happen to them."

Gosh, I thought. Dozens of couples in the Twin Cities would be interested in helping. We have money. Maybe we could pool our resources and create some kind of college fund. We can't help all these kids, but maybe we could help one or two a year.

"What can we do to help?" I asked.

"We have a student sponsorship program," Margaret responded. She promised to get me the information before we left.

The van took us back down the steep mountainside at the conclusion of the tour. The incline was hard on the vehicle; we could hear metal rubbing against raw metal as the driver applied the brakes.

"John," Margaret said, putting her arm around him in the third-row seat of the van. "Your country is in serious trouble. Do you know that?"

I listened a lot harder than John appeared to be. What did she mean by "your country?" John was a U.S. citizen. He was a part of my family. I prepared to interrupt, fearing she was about to dump a pile of adult problems on my 6-year-old.

"People are fighting in the countryside," Margaret said. "Many people have died. It is very serious. That is why we must all work for peace. And John, that means you too. You know where all violence starts? It starts in the home. You must be kind to your sisters and brother. Never argue with your parents. If we had peaceful homes around the world, we'd have no fighting."

* * *

That evening, Zuetana put on a big party in honor of two families that had received babies that day, and in honor of Paula and me since we'd be leaving early the next morning. A harpist provided music and while the hosts passed out cake and soda pop, Catherine danced by herself in the middle of the room. She bobbed from one foot to the other, and turned completely in a circle to the delight of other guests who had lined up in chairs around the perimeter of the room. John was seated on my left and Susan sat on my right with Michael on her lap. Paula was flitting from one adult to the next giving out hugs. Soon, other adults joined Catherine and by the time we all had been served a piece of cake, all the women and some of the men were dancing in a line with Catherine at the center.

I have never felt so at home as I felt at that moment. Our four kids were the shining light of the party. I loved them for having so much personality, for being so beautiful, for being so gracious with those around them, and for radiating so much joy. "You have a beautiful family," a Norwegian man told me. "Your kids are magnificent," said the French woman who earlier asked why we wanted four children. It was an easy moment for me to love the whole family. But as I looked at our kids – John with cake in his mouth, Paula hugging a newly made friend, Catherine dancing in her red dress, and Michael sleeping on mom's lap – I realized how much I had to credit Susan. I loved Susan for making all this happen. Oh sure, we both adopted these kids and we were parenting together, but it was really Susan who created this masterpiece that is the Bengtson family. Adoption was her idea in the first place. She was the one who made the calls, did the research, figured out what to do. I just did what she asked me to do, like my father told me. Now I was the father of my own beautiful family.

✳ ✳ ✳

Our driver arrived on time at 6:15 the next morning to take Paula and me to the airport. Although we planned for this moment, leaving was difficult. I hugged the three kids I would be leaving behind and kissed Susan goodbye. I turned away rather than watch the tears. On the ride to the airport, the wind from the open window dried any tears before they had a chance to roll down my cheek. I held Paula's hand the whole time, choosing to look outside rather than into her long face.

Paula and I sat quietly through the first few hours of the airplane ride. The airline had given us each headsets that we could plug into our armrest and listen to music. After consuming a 7-Up, Paula broke our long silence.

"What do you think my birth mom is doing right

now?" Paula asked.

What a question. "I really don't know," I said.

"Why did she give me up?"

"Paula, I am sure she loves you very much and wanted what she thought would be best for you. I am sure she looked at her own life, considered her options and decided adoption was the best route."

"I don't get it," Paula said, looking puzzled.

"Paula, you understand that your birth mother was very poor," I said, feeling more comfortable with this conversation than I expected. "You know that *barrio* we visited yesterday? That is the kind of neighborhood where your birth mother probably lives."

"Why is she poor?" Paula asked.

"Paula, there could be a million reasons. I can't even guess," I said. "But Paula, as you saw, there are thousands of people in the same situation."

"Is my birth mother okay?"

"I hope so. Keep in mind, she is a very young woman."

"What do you mean?"

"Well, your mother is probably in her early or mid twenties. You are nearly eight years old and she was only in her teens when she gave birth to you."

"What?!" Paula exclaimed. "You mean she was only as old as our baby sitter?"

"Yes."

"I can't believe that," Paula said. "I thought a mommy would be in her thirties, at least."

"Well, you are thinking of Susan. But there are girls who have babies at very young ages."

"Oh, I don't understand," Paula said.

"A lot of things are hard to understand when you are young," I said. "But you'll grow up. We all do."

She didn't ask any more questions.

I looked at Paula, who was lost in the music coming through her headset. I thought about Susan and the kids in Bogotá. I wondered how long it would be before we were all home.